FROM NOW ON...

FROM NOW ON...

RALPH SHALLIS

STL BOOKS

**PO Box 48, Bromley,
Kent, England
PO Box 28, Waynesboro,
Georgia 30830, USA**

© 1973 Ralph Shallis.

Translated and revised 1978, from the original French
title *Si tu veux aller loin*.

First British edition 1978, by STL Books.
Reprinted 1979, 1980, 1981, 1983, 1987.

STL Books are published by
Send The Light (Operation Mobilisation),
PO Box 48, Bromley, Kent, England.

ISBN 0 903843 17 X

Typesetting, production and printing by
Nuprint Ltd, Harpenden, Herts, AL5 4SE.

CONTENTS

THE AUTHOR

It was on the semi-desert plateau of Old Castile, in Spain, that Ralph Shallis grew up and first learned to think – in two languages! His childhood was lived – as he himself says – 'in the Middle Ages'. His later education took place in England, where, at the age of 18, he encountered God.

As a young man, teaching languages and literature in several different countries of Europe, he learned to integrate into a variety of cultures. But, already by the age of 23, he had become profoundly dissatisfied with his spiritual life, and was seeking a fresh revelation of God.

After studying the lives and work of a number of God's great men of previous generations, he grasped the fact that every one of them had an intimate knowledge of Christ that was beyond his own experience. He discovered that all these men, however different their characters and their work, had two secrets in common: thay all began the day in solitude with God in prayer; and they all read the whole Bible right through each year.

His thirst for God led him to follow their example. He undertook to read the Bible through in depth every year; and, to achieve this, and to have enough time for real prayer, he put aside a tenth of his time, that is, about two and a half hours a day, for God alone. This became a fundamental principle of life for him.

In those early days, Ralph Shallis was working in the Swiss Alps, and it was there, over the following three years, that the revelation of God's face became so overwhelming that life took on an altogether different meaning for him.

The Second World War then came as a terrible anti-climax, devouring five or six of the best years of his life. Yet, as a conscript soldier in Africa, Asia and Europe, he found his knowledge of God and man deepened by an extraordinary gamut of experiences and by the physical and spiritual suffering he had to face. During all that time, God enabled him to maintain his daily study of the Bible, and also kept him from taking life or doing evil to his fellow-men. The testing of his faith was severe, but it left him with no illusions about himself or human nature.

When he was finally free again, he resumed his teaching career, this time in Portugal. Here at last he was able to live with his young wife, Rangeley, whom he scarcely knew, even though they had been married for four years! But, now that he had seen the indescribable spiritual need of the world, he could no longer think of making a career for himself. With Rangeley, he decided, at the age of thirty-seven, to give all his time to Christ's service; and, together with their little family, they went to North Africa to make Christ known by any means they could, but most of all by diffusing the New Testament as widely as possible. This they did in total dependence on God, even for their daily bread – a simple faith that God has now honoured for well over a quarter of a century.

There, in suffering, poverty, and ignominy, they saw God bring into being a work of such spiritual potency that they were eventually overwhelmed and exhausted by the number of young men and others who came looking for Christ. The Algerian War tragically brought this evangelistic outreach to an end and scattered its fruits; but these have continued to multiply elsewhere. A number of those young men rose up to serve God mightily, and, through their work, especially in France, untold numbers of souls have been evangelised, new churches have come into being, and many other young men and women have been called to serve God.

For several years previous, Ralph Shallis had already been working in France and North Africa simultaneously; but now France became his main sphere of activity. Here, as in Africa, his heart opened wide to the spiritual needs of the younger generation. For him, this emphasis was a priority upon which the future of the world depends; and it was this that led him into an intimate co-operation with movements such as Operation Mobilisation. In recent years, the Spirit of God has driven him, not only over the whole of France, but to practically every country of Europe, and yet further afield – in almost every case in response to the cry of a young world thirsty for the reality of Christ.

In the streets and in universities, lecturing and by humble colportage, through sleepless nights and endless, deep personal discussions, he has had to come to grips with a vast range of urgent problems, facing up to the anguish of a generation no longer satisfied with mere religious theory or tradition, but wanting to discover the reality of God and the true meaning of life.

This book summarises the basic answers by which many lives have been transformed.

TO MY READER

This book is written for *you* as you begin that marvellous, but difficult, dangerous adventure that Jesus calls eternal life.

I hope you are young! Young at least in spirit. I haven't really written this book for the stolid old Christian who is convinced he has the whole bag of tools. Yet I believe that he too – if his charity can forgive my bluntness and if his faith can take a hard punch – will find something here to straighten out his thinking and jolt him into action!

Of course, I know this book is sure to find its way too into someone else's hands, someone who doesn't yet even know what the 'new birth' is all about. Well, I could hardly wish for anything better! Why not enter into the reality of this fantastic experience as you actually read through these pages? You will discover the meaning of heaven!

But in my heart of hearts I see my reader as a young disciple of Christ. I think of you as a baby just born into God's kingdom, yelling for food and needing to grow up desperately fast! It is for you really that I have written this book.

Of course, everybody loves a baby. Because (most of the time!) it is a delightful thing and lots of fun. Likewise, there is nothing more delightful on this earth than a new-born Christian. But when you meet someone who has remained a 'baby' for thirty or forty years, then you have something to weep about. My intense prayer is that you yourself will quickly get past the 'bottle-feeding' stage and be able to face up to a full spiritual 'beefsteak'! I want you to grow into tough, rich, spiritual maturity. I know you can, because God Himself wants it. So I have written this book to help you.

Like you, I am one of those amazingly privileged people whom God calls His children. I have been living in the

kingdom of God for over forty-five years. To help you gain
time and avoid some of the appalling blunders I have made
I want to hand over to you some of the weapons God has
forged for me over the years. You will need them.

I don't know what God intends to do with your life; but I
do know that, if you love Him enough to obey Him with
your whole heart, He will make it into something marvellous. The crucial question is this: what is your objective?
What in fact are you aiming at? A life of easy, sophisti-
cated comfort – a mediocre life that avoids the difficult but
supremely important issues? Or do you have your eyes on
God's limitless horizon?

You have a lifetime of exhilarating discovery before you.
The possibilities that God will achieve something wonderful
through you are infinite. His Spirit is not limited – except by
human unbelief. I pray your life will be a poem of sheer
dynamic beauty straight out of God's heart. I dare you to
come face to face with God.

Ralph Shallis,
Méjannes-les-Alès, France.

PREFACE TO THE ENGLISH EDITION

I find it rather a joke that this book was first written by me in a foreign language and then translated back into my own by someone else! I recognise in it something of the vast sense of humour that pervades all God's works, even the most exalted and solemn. I think that even my own funeral ought to be quite good fun – for me, at least! How can it be otherwise for somebody whose life is integrated into God Himself? No wonder Paul says, 'Rejoice!' – even on the cross. For if the light of God's presence floods our soul, we have discovered heaven and begun to live it even on this earth.

I wrote this book in French as a response to the eager and pathetic heartcry of thousands of young disciples of Christ, for whom no such work existed. To give them a solid and comprehensive basis for their life in Christ, the hand of God lay heavily upon me, and this was the result.

I had no thought, at least in the immediate future, of putting it into English, for the Christian market in the Anglo-Saxon world is inundated with books of every kind – 250 books, it is said, on the life of Paul! What a glut compared with the spiritual poverty of the rest of the world! So I felt it was folly to add to this abundance. Yet, so far as I know, nothing has been written even in English with the specific objective envisaged here. My intention is to make over to the young disciple of Christ what I call the *Seven Pillars of Divine Wisdom*. By this I mean the vital and essential secrets (but why are they secret?) by means of which a young believer can rapidly and steadily develop a life of spiritual fullness that is deeply grounded in the written Word of Christ. My supreme concern is that God shall raise up a generation of mighty men and women of God.

So God, true to His joyous sense of the unpredictable and

His love of paradox (of which Christ's life and teachings are so full), took the matter right out of my hands. Doris Coulston, for her own pleasure and that of her friends, translated my book into English quite independently of my own will. With the grace of Jesus, she sent me the manuscript, and she has allowed me to tinker with it to my heart's content. The result is, after all, a book by me! I have had the effrontery to rewrite the whole thing, reducing her beautifully precise translation into the possibly incoherent jumble of my own idiomatic style. So I can say that it is now a single work, like two roots grown into a single tree.

No words of mine can possibly repay Doris Coulston for this invaluable service she has rendered me, nor for the grace that inspired it. Nor can I ever express all the gratitude I feel to Connie Clarke (now Madame Daniel Waroux) for her selfless secretarial help, in both the French and the English editions, and without whom this book would certainly not exist. But my thanks go most of all to the Christ for whom all this has been attempted.

Spring 1978; Méjannes-les-Alès, France.

NOTE

The quotations from the Bible are taken as a rule from the Revised Standard Version. In some cases I have modified the text in order to interpret the Greek original more exactly; but in such cases I have normally mentioned the fact.

I believe the reader will gain by having a Bible or New Testament to hand, in which to study the Scriptures referred to in the footnotes.

INTRODUCTION

So the miracle has actually happened to you – you are born again! Think of it, you are now God's offspring! You are living in a new dimension; you are in possession of the treasure that Jesus calls 'eternal life'. In other words, *real* life; life that is rooted in God Himself, and therefore imperishable; life that nothing, not even physical death, can destroy. This new life or consciousness comes to you straight from the Source of all things, from the very Creator. Before that, you were spiritually dead, without any personal knowledge of God or any direct contact with Him; but now you are living in His very presence. You have discovered a new world, marvellous and radiant; and this extraordinary life doesn't merely surround you; it is also deep within you. The Spirit of God has come to dwell in you; He looks upon you as His house, His temple; He considers He is 'at home' there.

Of course, you are still living on the earth! This new inner existence does not detract from the reality of your physical and mental being. Indeed, far from stifling your human personality and your grasp of the surrounding world, this new life actually brings it all into focus. Everything becomes more real, more tangible; you begin to understand the true meaning of life. Colours are more vivid, experiences more positive; nature, science, beauty become an open book to you, a poem of God, unfathomably deep in meaning. Life, love, family and work have become infinitely more significant. For you, God is no longer a mere hypothesis or a myth; He penetrates all your thinking, and fills your heart. He is as real to you as the earth under your feet, or as the firm flesh on your fingers – perhaps even more real. This God, who was at one time unknown and even unknowable to you, has revealed His very heart to you in an outburst of unutterable love, expressed through His Son Jesus, once crucified for you, but now alive and powerful enough to deliver you!

In fact, you are living in two worlds at once, rather like a rose-bush, thoroughly rooted in the earth but at the same time existing in the air above. You still live in the everyday world, like everybody else, yet, simultaneously, you are living in the kingdom of God. Nothing has changed much in your day-to-day existence; you have the same human contacts and responsibilities as before, the same work and times of rest, the same studies, and the same times of weariness. But day and night you also have an intimate relationship with God.

The people around you simply can't understand; they can't fathom what is happening inside you. Even though nature shouts aloud in their ears the very beauty and wisdom of God, even though science is crammed full of spiritual analogies, people often take you for a poor visionary. People don't like what they can't understand. Yet, for you, everything is as clear as crystal. Before it happened, you were blind; now you can see. Formerly, you did not know God, but now He is utterly real to you, intimately so, on the deepest personal level. He who is the fantastically intelligent Source of the vast energy of the whole universe has become your Father, your 'Daddy' – that is the gist of Paul's expression in Aramaic, 'Abba, Father'.[1] Like the rose-bush, you are fully involved in the earthly existence in which you are still rooted, but you are intensely aware also of living in the celestial atmosphere of God. You gaze into the unfathomable blue of his heaven; you are blessed with light from the radiance of His face; you drink in the great wind of His Spirit that sweeps over you. You can't expect the rose to flower under the soil; neither can the natural man expect to grasp the things of God. To do that, you have to be born again, *'from above'*, as Jesus expresses it. So now Christ's life begins to blossom out through you into a new personality.

I can understand you, because I have travelled the same way. Like you, I am a child of God,[2] and therefore your

(1) Rom. 8:15

(2) No allusion to the modern sect that calls itself 'The Children of God'. I have no sympathy with the moral degradation that characterises its doctrines and practices. See the Report of the Public Attorney of the State of New York, as reported in the *Daily Telegraph* (15th October 1974).

brother. My own experience of this life, so far from disintegrating or losing its meaning, goes on developing year by year and day after day. God has continued to give me fresh, overwhelming revelations of Himself, things inexpressible and beyond human imagination.

So I am offering you a lifetime of discovery and experience compressed into this brief book, things learned in ecstasy and grief, and also by dint of sheer, slogging work.

My desire, my prayer, is that the hand of God will fashion you, beginning this very day, into a man or woman of God. That, I know, is the very thing God longs for.

Part I

FAILURE – OR AN EXPLOSIVE FULLNESS?

1

THE INITIAL SHOCK

Your Three Enemies

What a surprise! It is just as if you've had a fist right in your face. After discovering God, now you have discovered evil.

This is what I mean: before our new birth, we were all more or less conscious of the existence of evil. Wars, famines, concentration camps, pollution, corruption, broken homes – all these things did indeed trouble us. But now we are born again, we see everything in the stark light of God's face, and evil assumes frightening proportions. We become conscious of it as never before. We are intensely grieved as we perceive the true state of the world, the unbelievable follies of mankind, the delight men take in doing evil, their ignorance of God, their lack of a spiritual horizon. We wish that everyone could understand what we have discovered; our heart is broken with the suffering of God, with the pain we see expressed in Christ crucified, with the love of God for the world that has rejected Him. We begin to realise the full extent of evil and to understand its true nature.

As for you, because you now belong to God, you find the forces of evil actually arrayed against you. They cannot conquer you, for Christ is stronger than they are; but they are powerful and dangerous. You need to know their strategy and confront them with weapons forged by God. There are a number of things you *must* understand.

Evil proceeds from three sources: from the 'devil', the 'world', and the 'flesh'.

Your first enemy : The Devil

The Middle Ages bequeathed to us a concept of the devil which is quite false and even ridiculous. People often think of him as a more or less mythological being, duly equipped with horns and living quite happily in hell, from whence he emerges from time to time to prod us into committing some sin or other. But how different is the Bible teaching on this subject!

You need at this stage to read Ezekiel 28:12–19 and Isaiah 14:12–14. These two passages give us a glimpse of a satanic power controlling the nations. They tell us that this dangerous being was created by God originally without sin, and that he was the most powerful of all spirits, a creature of extraordinary beauty and intelligence. He was even the guardian 'cherub' protecting the intimacy of God's presence. But 'his heart became proud because of his beauty'; he was not content with his position, he wanted to be 'like the Most High'. From that moment, he was 'driven out' and lost his fellowship with God.

Nevertheless – we don't quite know why – God has allowed him to retain his liberty and even his position of vast authority over this planet for the time being. In spite of that, he has become God's implacable enemy (his name 'Satan' means 'the enemy'), knowing that the day is coming when he will be flung into the abyss and finally into hell itself.[1] The everlasting fire has been prepared especially for him and his angels; the people who follow him will inevitably share his fate.[2]

This terrible being has, it appears, dragged with him in his fall a third of the angels of God.[3] He still has access to heaven,[4] and, in that invisible world, he fights against the angels of God and accuses the disciples of Christ.[5] (The word 'devil' means 'slanderer'; that is, the accuser who attacks from behind.) He controls a vast demonic hierarchy in the heavenly places, which we have to confront with the seven-fold armour of God;[6] which, however, does not include any defence for the man who turns his back on the enemy! The devil goes around seeking whom he may devour, but we must resist him with a firm faith, and he will eventually give way

(1) Rev. 20:1–3, 10
(2) Mt. 25:41
(3) Rev. 12:4
(4) Job 1:6–12
(5) Rev. 12:7–10
(6) Eph. 6:11–18

before us;[7] for He who is in us is greater than he who is in the world.[8]

Satan's chief objective is not necessarily to tempt people to 'sin', but *to turn them from the truth of Christ*, for it is through Christ alone that we can gain a true idea of God. Satan wants to warp the 'image' of God in men's thinking, *so that he may pass himself off as God*. He has never changed his objective: he wants to be 'like the Most High'. It matters little to him whether a man is a philosopher or an ignoramus, a respectable citizen or a dissolute outcast, or even whether he is a religious man or an atheist. What he is concerned about is the blinding of that man to the truth of the Lord Jesus Christ.[9] He is utterly ruthless.

Your second enemy : The World

The Bible draws a clear distinction between the 'earth' and the 'world'. When God created the earth, He pronounced all His work to be 'very good'.[10] By the *earth*, the Scripture means our material planet with its marvellous beauty and its countless forms of life, reflecting the greatness of the Creator and his deep joy in all his workmanship.[11] God placed the first man and woman in the garden of this earth and called them, *as a couple*, his 'image',[12] saying that this was 'very good'. Oh, the incredible beauty of marriage as God first conceived it – and what a tragedy that the Fall should have intervened!

Christian theology, from the third century onwards, was deeply influenced by Greek philosophy, and especially by Neoplatonism, which introduced the idea of an antagonism between soul and matter. Proceeding almost certainly from Asia, it taught that only the soul is pure while matter is essentially evil. It is still today the basic doctrine of Hinduism and Buddhism; it accounts for the asceticism and also for the immorality of Europe in the Middle Ages, as well as other anomalies in Christian history. This idea is, however,

(7) Jas. 4:7; 1 Pet. 5:8
(8) 1 Jn. 4:4
(9) 2 Cor. 3:14; 4:3–4
(10) Gen. 1:31
(11) Rom. 1:20; Prov. 8:30–31
(12) Gen. 1:27

in flagrant contradiction with God's thought; for, having created matter and life, he pronounced them *good*.

The *world*, according to the Bible, is quite another thing; it is thoroughly evil. The Biblical expression 'the world' (Greek: cosmos[13]) occasionally means 'the heavens and the earth' or 'the universe', the vast cosmic system created by God; but in the New Testament it nearly always means the *world system* which men have built up for themselves and which God condemns. It is not subject to the authority of God; it even permeates the earth, which it pollutes, spoils and destroys with its folly and its injustices.

The Bible reveals the astonishing and terrifying truth that the god of this world is Satan.[14] He is also called 'the prince of the power of the air' and 'the spirit that is now at work in the children of disobedience'.[15] Jesus calls him 'the prince of this world', and adds that he has already been judged – thank God for that![16] Since his desire is to be 'like the Most High', he encourages and inspires man in the creation of an advanced civilisation, in the development of the arts and sciences and even of religion, as in this way he can attract to himself a glory like that of God. When men, consciously or unconsciously, attribute these things to him, he has achieved his objective: he has obliterated the true idea of God from the world of men's thought, and put his own image in its place.

This does not mean, of course, that there is no place for *true* art and science, which reveal God to the world. It is simply a tragic fact that most of this world's genius leads away from Christ into the dark. There is, in fact, a great need for Christian poets, philosophers, painters, composers, scientists and technicians. We have been too slow to realise this.

Since men reject the true God, of whom Jesus Christ is the only valid portrait, they inevitably worship or admit the existence of another god, the one who is His enemy. Paul says that Satan has blinded the minds of the unbelievers in order to prevent their understanding the good news of

(13) The Greek word *aiōn* (aeon or age) is also often used to describe 'this world'.

(14) 2 Cor. 4:4

(15) Eph. 2:2

(16) Jn. 12:31; 14:30; 16:11

Christ.[17] John says that the whole world is under the power of the evil one.[18] Therefore it is not to be wondered at if God forbids us to love the world; for, 'if anyone loves the world, the love of the Father is not in him'.[19] Jesus warned his disciples, saying: 'If the world hates you, you know that it hated me before it hated you.'[20]

Let us get this quite clear: we have to understand that the world is our enemy. It has no place for Jesus. At His birth, the world pushed Him into a stable; and, when He reached the flower of His manhood, it condemned Him as a criminal, insulted Him, humiliated Him, and finally tortured Him to death, nailing Him up on a tree trunk.

On the other hand, the *earth*, in spite of its exploitation by man and its labouring under the satanic curse resulting from Adam's fall, is still a joy to the child of God. Each flower, each dawn, each living creature is, for him, a miracle of divine wisdom. But he sees the *world* as a tragedy, an agonising spectacle, an insidious danger. Ah yes! At one time, he felt quite at home in the world; but now everything is different. He realises that he no longer belongs to its system or its god. He belongs to another kingdom, the kingdom of God.

God says: 'Do not love the world or the things in the world.'[21] But Jesus also said: 'Be of good cheer! I have overcome the world.[22] And yet again: 'God so loved the world that he gave his Son . . .'[23]

There are two very different ways of loving the world! We cannot love its evil system, but we cannot do otherwise than love the souls of the men and women caught in the machinery.

Your third enemy : The evil within you[24]

But, worst of all, the thing that really shocks us is the discovery of the presence of evil within us personally, *in spite*

(17) 2 Cor. 4:4
(18) 1 Jn. 5:19
(19) 1 Jn. 2:15
(20) Jn. 15:18
(21) 1 Jn. 2:15–17
(22) Jn. 16:33
(23) Jn. 3:16
(24) Rom. 7:7–21

of the new birth. We are saddened and profoundly humiliated
to find that we are still capable of sinning. We are conscious
of thoughts, words and deeds that do not glorify God. We
are deeply troubled by it, and quite rightly. Some of God's
children even reach the point of doubting their salvation
because of it. How, they ask themselves, can a child of God
still sin? In fact, our moral consciousness has been made
extremely sensitive by the Spirit and the Word of God. We
begin to recognise a whole gamut of sins of which, only
yesterday, we were quite unconscious, or which we tolerated
quite comfortably. But now we are crushed under a sense of
depravity and guilt as we look at the Christ who paid for our
spiritual bankruptcy at the cost of His very blood.

The Two Slaveries

Well, take courage, for even the Apostle Paul himself,
in his writings, confesses that even he has the very same
problem! In this context you really must make a special
study of his marvellous letter to the Romans, particularly
of chapters 6–8. In this great passage he analyses the problem
in depth and shows us the divine solution. These chapters
are among the most profound writings in all the literature of
the world. You can spend a whole lifetime studying them
without exhausting their meaning; you continually discover
more riches in them and an ever-deeper significance. So you
need to start young on the job!

In chapter 7, where Paul describes his anguish over the
conflict within his own soul, he is speaking of the power of
sin. In chapter 8, he describes the all-powerful work of the
Spirit of God which conquers sin in his life. He fully recognises the power of sin, he does not minimise it; but he
insists that the power of God is greater. Then, in chapter 6,
the Apostle Paul speaks of two slaveries: slavery to God
and slavery to sin.

The fact is, sin is stronger than we are. Whether we admit
it or not, man *is* a slave. He is mastered by a 'virus' that has
invaded his whole being; it is the devastating, destroying
growth that the Bible calls 'sin'. It is a spiritual cancer, a
deadly disease against which not even the strongest man in
the world can stand. A single, microscopic leukaemia cell in
the blood is enough to take away all a man's hope and destroy
him: it is stronger than the man himself.

Sin is a deadly slavery from whose power it is quite impossible to escape – except by changing masters! When I acknowledge the authority of Jesus Christ in my life, and give him every right over my being, *then* the power of sin is broken. Paradoxically enough, I then also become free – not by my own effort, for I can never by my own power break the authority of sin. But I am freed from that authority by a force that is greater than that of sin: I am freed by the Christ who is now living in me. My will, liberated at last from the conflict, discovers its true purpose as my existence becomes integrated into that of my Creator.

Deliverance is an Act of God

There is nothing we can do to 'get born again', nor can we ever deserve God's pardon; we have to accept His pardon, like birth itself, as a pure gift. We don't create our own life, it just comes to us. Neither can we do anything about delivering ourselves from the power of sin. Our only way out is to accept deliverance as a free gift from God. The Spirit of God never forces a sinner to be converted; He leaves him free to accept or to refuse. He likewise respects the will of the believer; He does not force anyone to be sanctified! As soon as we give Him the right to act, He works.

The functioning of the Spirit of God is like the sap rising in the tree; it flows out through the branches, creating the leaves, flowers, fruit and seed, thus enabling the tree to reproduce itself. In the springtime, as this miracle begins to operate, a vast ferment of energy is liberated; yet we do not see the tree making any visible effort whatsoever! The life-process works itself out in apparent silence. So, in the same way, the Holy Spirit produces the life of Christ in us *spontaneously*, creating the flower of His character, out of which develops the fruit of spiritual maturity.

2

YOUR INNER CONFLICT

The Paradox of the Two Natures

The New Testament teaches very clearly that the child of God has two distinct 'personalities' or 'natures'. As we study the epistles of Paul, we sense the difficulty he experienced in finding words to express these things. It was the first time in the world's history that anyone had tried to define them. Writing as the Spirit of God inspired him, he finally chose certain quite everyday words, but lifted them into a new dimension, infusing a heavenly and spiritual meaning into them. In this short chapter we cannot explore all the depths of these marvellous truths, but I hope at least we can clarify them.

Saul and Paul

Before reading what follows, it would be advisable for you to look very carefully at Romans 7:14–25, the better to grasp this explanation. Paul says in verse 15: 'I do not understand my own actions. For I do not do what I want, but I do the very thing I hate.' So, in a way, there are two Pauls speaking. You will remember that, before his conversion, Paul was named Saul. With that in mind, we can re-read the whole of this passage making a clear distinction between 'Saul' and 'Paul', between the old 'Saul', the natural man before his conversion, and the new 'Paul', the child of God who had met Christ on the Damascus road. These two personalities co-exist in the same man. Paul says: 'I . . . I . . . '; but at one moment he is thinking of Saul, and the next of Paul. So I suggest we re-read this passage as follows; 'I (Saul) do not do what I (Paul) want, but I (Saul) do what I (Paul) hate. Therefore if I (Saul) do what I (Paul) do not want, I (Paul) agree that the law is good; so then it is no longer I (Paul) that do it, but the sin which dwells within me (Saul).' Verse 21: 'So I find it to be a law (or principle) that, when I (Paul) want to do right, evil is present with (or in) me (Saul);[1] for I delight in the law of God in my inmost self (Paul), but I see in my members another law (or authority, or principle) at war with the law (or authority) of my mind and which makes me (Saul) captive to the law (or authority) of sin which is in my members.'

Then Paul cries out in verse 24: 'Wretched man that I am! Who will deliver me from the body (or, better translated, "from the power or substance or reality") of this death?' But he finishes triumphantly: 'Thank God! It is by Jesus Christ our Lord (that I am delivered).' That, I believe, is the meaning of this passage.

So Paul recognises a real conflict of the two personalities within himself: the old nature, utterly hostile to the law or authority of God, refusing to submit to His will; and the new nature, born of God, actually longing to do His will and live according to His law.

Every true Christian experiences the same thing. After the new birth, he discovers a terrible conflict within himself. He does, in fact, have two 'personalities', or rather, *natures*. The old one never did care about God, and even now it totally rejects His will. The Bible says that it is incurably evil and deceitful above all things.[2] The New Testament teaches insistently that this old nature is beyond recovery; it cannot be either improved or reformed. Whereas all the world's religions and philosophies try to boost up this old nature, God totally refuses to take it into account. He insists on beginning all over again. He is satisfied with nothing less than the creation of a new life, the complete refashioning of your personality. He wants to give you a new heart.[3]

The seed and the earth : A remarkable analogy

Nature is rich in illustrations of spiritual truth. The earth of itself is dead and cannot produce life. For that, it depends on the seed that falls into it; for the seed, as it germinates and grows, transforms the dead soil into a living plant. A rose-

(1) This could almost be translated 'evil clings to me'.
(2) Jer. 17:9
(3) Ezek. 36:26–27

tree or an oak is entirely composed of earth – dead, inert
earth, which the life-principle of the seed has seized upon,
integrating it into a new, living organism. Just as God said
that man is dust, so the tree is indeed composed of nothing
but dust. Yet it is not the earth that makes the tree; it is the
life-principle itself that changes the earth into a tree.

God tells us that, just as the earth in itself is incapable of
producing life, so our old nature is incapable of doing God's
will or even of desiring to do it. But, in our dead soul, God
now plants the seed of life, that is to say, His living Word,
which is Christ, revealed in the written Word. And this seed,
quickened by the 'water' of the Spirit of God, lays hold of the
elements of our old, dead personality, transforming them
into a new, living personality, created in the image of Christ.
That is the miracle of the new birth.

Life in another dimension

So you have two personalities within you. You are Saul,
but also Paul! You will never be able to change Saul's nature,
you will never be able to make it into anything of value for
God. On the other hand, your new personality does want at
all costs to do the will of God, and in fact cannot do anything
else. Paul describes it in these astonishing words; 'It is
Christ who lives in me'.[4] This new life has its source in God
Himself. God calls it His child; and, of course, the child
resembles his Father.

The old nature is always in rebellion against God. When
you sin, it is your old nature that sins, not the new one. When
you do the will of God, it is your new nature that does it,
never the old nature. What a marvellous thought! Your new
nature is incapable of sinning! 'He who is born of God,' John
tells us, 'does not sin and actually cannot sin.'[5] But he says
also that we make God a liar and we deceive ourselves if we
claim to be without sin![6] At first sight John seems to be
contradicting himself; but in fact he is doing nothing of the
sort. John, like Paul, recognises the existence of a real inner
conflict in the believer's soul.

(4) Gal. 2:20
(5) 1 Jn. 3:9–10
(6) 1 Jn. 1:8, 10

The Christian is not a schizophrenic. His 'old' nature is not divided; it is perfectly 'normal' by worldly standards. The explanation of his dilemma lies in the fact that he now possesses a wholly new life, he exists in a dimension beyond the experience of other men. Like a man who has lived in the heart of the desert, or climbed Mount Everest, or been to the moon, he knows a world as yet beyond the grasp of other men.

People around us simply don't understand anything of all this, and, of course, there is no vocabulary in ordinary speech to describe such experiences. 'Man has no heavenly language', said a certain wise man. God has had to create a whole new terminology for us, through which to communicate the truths that lie beyond our natural comprehension. And this is what He has done in the Bible.

The biblical terminology

Before we end this chapter, it will be useful to take note of the expressions God has used in the New Testament to describe the two natures of the believer. The old, evil personality is called *the old man*, or *the sin which dwells in me*, or *sin in the flesh*; sometimes it is called simply *sin*, or just *the flesh*. This last expression appears very often in Paul's writings; but it must not be confused with the word *body*, for which the Greek word is quite different. According to Paul, the *body* of the believer, even though still mortal, is actually the temple of the Holy Spirit; but *the flesh* is the very root of sin, not only in the human body, but in the soul as well. It is the infectious 'sin-principle' that has pervaded and tormented the whole human race since man first fell. At the return of Christ, in our resurrected body, we shall be forever rid of this evil principle; even its very root will disappear. The old nature will cease to exist. What a relief!

The new nature also has several names in the New Testament. Among others, we find *the new man*, *the inward man*, *the divine nature*, *he who is born of God*, *Christ who lives in me*. But the expression most frequently used in Paul's writings is *the spirit*, generally printed in our Bibles with a small *s*. When the New Testament was written, of course, the original Greek made no distinction between capital and small letters, so it is not surprising if, in a few passages, it is not always easy at first sight to decide whether the word *spirit* refers to the Spirit of God or to the regenerate human spirit. I think God has deliberately allowed this margin of ambiguity in order to emphasise the intimate and inextricable relationship that now exists between the Spirit of God and our spirit – in Christ. There is almost something of divine confusion between the two – heavenly thought! That is why the Apostle Paul says: 'Who can separate us from the love of God?'[7]

What a difference between soul and spirit!

Greek philosophy exalted the 'soul' above everything else. But, as God sees it, the soul of man is dead – unless it possesses what the Bible calls 'spirit'. The 'natural' man, even at his best, and even if he is the greatest scientific genius, is incapable of understanding the things of God because they can be discerned only *spiritually*.[8] He lacks that *spiritual* sense which would enable him to know God, *Who is Spirit*.[9] His soul's upreach is limited by a 'ceiling' of spiritual unconsciousness beyond which he cannot penetrate.

In the Bible, the word *soul* (in Hebrew *nephesh* and in Greek *psychè*) means 'breath', just as does the word *spirit* (Hebrew *rouach;* Greek *pnuema*). But God sets them in such complete contrast that he does not hesitate to describe wisdom that is merely intellectual and lacks love as earthly, 'soulish' (RSV *unspiritual*, Greek *psychikè*), and 'demoniacal' (Greek *daimoniodès*).[10] On the other hand, the soul of the child of God becomes impregnated, through his reborn spirit, by the action of the Spirit of God progressively enlightening and transforming the thinking-process of the soul.

So a solution does exist to the problem of your inner conflict, but it is a miraculous one. The new birth itself is miraculous; it is the beginning of eternal life, and eternal life is an unending miracle.

(7) Rom. 8:35
(8) 1 Cor. 1:18–25; 2:14–15
(9) Jn. 4:24
(10) Jas. 3:15. See also Jude 19

3

YOU – THE TEMPLE OF THE HOLY SPIRIT?

Could you have even imagined such a thing? You are in very truth the temple of God! The Spirit of God is now actually living within you. How could anyone believe such an audacious thought if the Word of God did not so bluntly state it? But the New Testament has in fact at least thirty passages saying with stark clarity that every child of God is the dwelling-place of the Holy Spirit. Here are some of them:

1 Corinthians 6:19: 'Don't you know that your body is the temple of the Holy Spirit, who is in you, and whom you have from God?'

In this single verse Paul says *three times over* that the Christians in Corinth had the Holy Spirit within them. He does not make any distinction here between those who were spiritually strong and those who were weak; he is speaking of all of them. Moreover, this passage doesn't refer only to the Christians in Corinth, but also to 'all that in every place call upon the name of Jesus Christ our Lord', as Paul makes clear in his introduction.[1]

It is a fact that the majority of the members of the church at Corinth were very imperfect. Paul reproves them for quite a number of serious faults, including quarrelling, divisions, lawsuits, and even the tolerating of a really bad case of immorality among them. There was actually disorder at the Lord's table, and real doctrinal confusion, some even going so far as to disbelieve in the resurrection. Paul charges them with being 'carnal' believers, spiritual 'babies'.[2] Nevertheless, he does not hesitate to say that they have the Holy Spirit indwelling them. This verse alone[3] would be sufficient

(1) 1 Cor. 1:2
(2) 1 Cor. 3:1, 2
(3) chapter 6, v. 19

to place beyond any doubt the fact that each true child of God, however weak, has the Holy Spirit within him.

In *1 Corinthians 3:16* Paul says once more to the same church: 'Don't you know you are the temple of God, and that the Spirit of God dwells in you?'

In *2 Corinthians 6:16* he says both of himself and of the Christians of Corinth: 'We are the temple of the living God.'

In *1 Thessalonians 4:8* to the Christians of Thessalonica, Paul says: 'God has also given you His Spirit.'

In *Romans 8:9–11*, Paul equates the Spirit of God with the Spirit of Christ and insists: 'Anyone who does not have the Spirit of Christ does not belong to Him.'[4]

How exhilarating! If God himself had not said it, I would never have dared believe He would condescend to come and live within me, calling me His dwelling-place!

But there is something else even more astonishing in this New Testament teaching: God says that not only our heart, but our very *body* is the temple of the Holy Spirit. What a privilege! My friend, as you walk down the street, you can be proud! You can confidently say to yourself that God is walking along the road with you, even within you. The Eternal One, Who created the universe and holds all things in being, Who is the source of all intellect and all energy, is in you, continuously animating your whole being. He is there for the avowed purpose of fulfilling Himself in your life, of living through you!

But who is the Holy Spirit?

For many people, this is still a very mysterious subject; it has been all too often ignored or misunderstood in the churches, and the whole question is even now surrounded with almost unbelievable confusion. Yet the Bible gives us very clear and full teaching about the Holy Spirit; if you read the whole of God's Book carefully, you cannot but be convinced of it.

The Holy Spirit is God – the Bible leaves us in no doubt

(4) For those who want to make a deeper study of this subject, here are some other interesting passages. Rom. 5:5; 8:15, 16, 23, 26–27; 1 Cor. 2:12; 12:3, 7; 2 Cor. 1:21–22; 5:5; Gal. 3:2, 5, 14; 4:6; 5:25; Eph. 1:13, 14; 4:30; Col. 2:10; 1 Thess. 4:8; 2 Tim. 1:7, 14; Titus 3:5, 6; James 4:5; 1 John 3:24; 2:20, 27; 4:13; 5:10

about that! Thus we are brought into the very heart of the greatest of all mysteries, that of the Trinity. The actual word *Trinity* is not found in the Scriptures. It was introduced into Christian vocabulary long after the apostolic era, to help define the Biblical truth about God, and to refute the heresies that had grown up about the person of Christ and that of the Holy Spirit. But the doctrine of the Trinity is, in fact, most clearly taught in the Bible, and I would like to emphasise one of its aspects.

We read that God is Love.[5] There is no doubt that God created the universe because He wanted to express his overwhelming love and also because He sought the love of intelligent beings such as men and angels. But whom or what could God possibly have loved before the universe existed? You can't love nothing; indeed, love cannot exist if there is nothing to love! Since God *is* love, we must understand that love is bound up in His very existence. If He didn't love, He would not be God; He would not exist; in fact, nothing would exist. This means that, even before creating the universe, He necessarily contains[6] within Himself the Object of His love, and this He calls His Son. Between the Father and the Son there is a reciprocal, eternal, unchangeable love.

God longs to make His love known to all the intelligent beings He has created. But man cannot of himself fathom the depths of God's heart. This is possible only if God takes the initiative and Himself reveals and communicates His thought. Yet this He does by the *Word*. Jesus Christ is called, in the Bible, the Word of God. He is the expression of the thought of God, which is perfect love.

The breath of God

However, a mere word is inaudible if it is not vocalised, that is, unless it is given 'body' or sound by means of the breath. So man cannot hear or understand the divine Word unless God 'breathes' or 'vocalises' it – that is, 'speaks' His thought. When God accompanies His Word with the energy

(5) 1 Jn. 4:8, 16

(6) I say 'contains' because in God there can be no past or future. His self-definition is: *I am.*

of His 'Breath', that is to say, His Spirit, that marvellous Word becomes intelligible to man's consciousness. Heaven opens to him as he discovers the infinite love of God.

The word *spirit* comes from the Latin *spiritus*, which literally means the breath. *Spiritus* is in turn the translation of the Greek word *pneuma* which means exactly the same thing. You can translate it as either *wind, breath* or *spirit*. In English we distinguish between spirit and breath; but there is no such distinction in Latin or Greek; they both use the same word for either thought. We see this quite clearly in John 3:5–8, where Jesus, saying that the wind blows wherever it wishes, is referring at the same time to the activity of the Spirit of God; in each case the Greek word used in the original text of the passage is *pneuma*.

Thus the Holy Spirit is the Breath of God, just as Jesus is the Son and the Word of God. While the word expresses the thought of the heart, the breath renders this word audible. The 'Son' of God *is actually God expressing Himself*, speaking His unfathomable Word, demonstrating the joy of His love; and, likewise, the 'Spirit' of God *is God making this Word audible*, rendering it intelligible to man. It would be interesting to go deeply into this truth, but it isn't possible to say everything in a book of this size!

It is God working in you

So, as the Spirit of God breathes upon you, He speaks into your soul the very thought of God's heart; acting thus upon you, He fashions the image of Christ in your own consciousness. His first desire is to reveal Christ *to* you; after that, He wants to express Him *through* you. For, once you have accepted the light, you yourself become a source of light. God begins to radiate outwards through your life; you become a reflection of His love.

When you open your heart to God, His Spirit enters. Just as the light of spring causes the earth to spring into flower, just as a girl's face can overturn the heart of a young man when the revelation of love dawns upon him, so the Holy Spirit engenders the very life of Christ in you as He breaks into your soul. Before that, you were dead in your sins,[7] but the next moment your dead spirit revives; you are

(7) Eph. 2:1

born from above, your soul receives sight, and you find yourself contemplating the miracle of eternal beauty. You begin to look straight into the face of God. You are a baby just born into the kingdom of light, you are the youngest member of God's family!

A real miracle has come to pass in you, the miracle that God calls the new birth. It is the beginning of eternal life. And all this, the New Testament teaches, is the work of the Holy Spirit. It is He who creates the likeness of Christ in your soul. It is He who writes the law of God into your heart, and transforms your whole concept of life. It is He who engenders the love of God in you, and who reveals the glory of God to you in the face of Jesus Christ. You are beginning to understand the meaning of heaven in your own experience.

And what then?

'Having begun with [Greek: by means of] the Spirit,' says Paul,[8] 'are you now ending with [by means of] the flesh?' It is the Spirit of God who began this fantastic work in you, and He alone can develop it. Paul adds:[9] 'Since we now live [have received life] by means of the Spirit, let us also walk [that is, go on, advance, thrust forward] by means of the Spirit.' It just isn't possible to live the Christian life on this earth except by the power of God's Spirit, any more than you can become a child of God without Him. No one can 'get himself born'. No one can 'get himself to grow' either. It is all the work of God. It is all supernatural.

(8) Gal. 3:3
(9) Gal. 5:25

4

THE FULLNESS OF
THE SPIRIT

The real life of a disciple of Jesus

'*Be filled with the Spirit*'[1] Every child of God is indwelt by the Holy Spirit, but not every child of God has the fullness of the Spirit. Too often people think that this fullness is a spiritual 'luxury', reserved for a few exceptionally privileged believers. But God most ardently wants us all to be 'filled with all the fullness of God', an experience that Paul identifies with 'the knowledge of the love of Christ which surpasses all knowledge'![2] Few Christians seem to understand this. Mostly they seem content to jog along with a mediocre or rather poor spiritual life. But in God's sight, the fullness of the Spirit is not a luxury: it is a *necessity*. God insists on it. 'Be filled with the Spirit' is a *command*. To remain unfilled is therefore not merely abnormal: it is sin.

Through the new birth you enter into the kingdom of God – but why stay at the frontier? The God who has saved you from hell isn't going to abandon you after that by the wayside! Since God is infinite, eternal life inevitably has unlimited possibilities. Why limit His Spirit by unbelief? Aim high!

The two levels of Christian experience

God draws a vivid distinction between the spiritual and the carnal Christian.[3] The carnal Christian is like a baby still 'on the bottle'! His spiritual senses are insufficiently developed to explore the 'deep things' of God.[4] As a spiritual

(1) Eph. 5:18
(2) Eph. 3:14–19
(3) 1 Cor. 3:1–3; Heb. 5:11–14
(4) 1 Cor. 2:9–12

infant, he gets stuck at the ABC stage; whereas the grown man, the adult believer, can discern between good and evil and is capable of teaching others about the things of God.

Paul tells us that some believers have their minds set on the things of God and that others have theirs set on the things of the flesh.[5] The spiritual Christian is the man who makes over all his rights to God; he pins his faith in Christ *for everything;* he sets out to do God's will with his whole heart. God can fill or possess such a man and use him to the uttermost. The carnal Christian, on the other hand, is always being attracted by the things of the world, and even by sin. He neglects the means God has given him for the deepening of his spiritual life. He remains pitifully weak, vacillating right and left in the wake of all sorts of unprofitable things. He is in a state of continual suffering and distress, because, deep down, he knows the truth and he really does love God. Inwardly, he wants to do God's will; but he finds in his daily experience that he is often incapable of it. He is a child of God, but still immature; he hasn't grown up. A new-born baby, as we have already said, is a most attractive thing; but a 'baby' of forty years old is far from a joke. It is a horror, a pitiable and even repulsive object. The spiritual Christian is one who is filled with the Spirit of God. The carnal Christian has the Spirit of God in him and 'with' him, otherwise he would not be a child of God; but he lacks the vitality, the overwhelming abundance of the *fullness* of the Spirit.

The difference between installation and repairs !

I can best explain the difference between these two spiritual 'levels' by an analogy. Imagine two houses side by side. They have the same water and electricity installations. In one of the houses, the installation is in good shape; when you need it, you can have as much light or water as you want and when you want it. In the other house there are electricity failures and leaking pipes. When you turn on the tap, you get nothing but a mere trickle of water; if you press the switch you discover the light bulb is broken and no one has bothered to replace it. Yet both houses have the same supplies of water

(5) Rom. 8:5–7

and electricity! The difference lies in the state of repair of each house.

You see, the carnal Christian *could* have as much blessing as any one, but in fact he does not benefit from that continual abundance which makes the spiritual Christian what he is. He desperately needs to call in the divine 'Plumber' or 'Electrician' to come and put his installation into working-order!

The real purpose of the fullness of the Spirit

God gives us the fullness of His Spirit *for the doing of His will*, and His will is essentially that Christ may be revealed to lost souls.

There are two facets to this truth. We see first of all, as we read the Acts of the Apostles, that the disciples are frequently filled with the Holy Spirit, and from these passages we discern clearly that the chief purpose of this fullness is *to make their witness for Christ effective*. Thus, on the day of Pentecost,[6] they are able to convince and convert no less than three thousand people. Later on, Peter,[7] facing the authorities responsible for the crucifixion of his Master, denounces their crime with astonishing courage. Then, coming out of prison,[8] Peter and John speak the Word of God with boldness (the Greek word means 'audacity'). We read also that Barnabas, Paul's colleague, is a man full of the Holy Spirit,[9] and that Paul brazenly rebukes Elymas, the sorcerer friend of the dictator of Cyprus, and binds his demonic powers.[10]

In all these cases we see that the Spirit of God, in His fullness, invests the word and witness of the apostles with the *very authority of God*. They knew, from what Christ had told them, that the Holy Spirit would come with the specific intention of making Him known.[11] This is evident from the statement in Acts 4:32–33: 'With great power the apostles witnessed to the resurrection of the Lord Jesus.' So the Spirit fills you *in order to witness through you* to the world about Christ, to convince men that He is the Truth.

(6) Acts 2
(7) Acts 4:8
(8) Acts 4:31
(9) Acts 11:24
(10) Acts 13:9
(11) Jn. 15:26–27; 16:13–15

In the second place we learn, from this same book of the Acts, that the Holy Spirit came *to unite all Christ's disciples in a single, closely-knit body;* He came *to fill them with love.* This supernatural love was the weapon He used to convince the world, the instrument through which He witnessed to the reality of Jesus.[12] Christ has promised that the world will indeed believe if only we, His disciples, love one another as He has loved us, with that intensity of love He showed us at the cross. *This presence of Jesus in our midst is the vital factor in our witness and it comes from the Spirit of God.* We read: 'The company of those who believed were of one heart and soul . . . they had everything in common . . . and great grace was upon them all.'[13]

What *is* the fullness of the Spirit?

As the size of this book does not allow me to deal with this subject in depth, I can only offer you a brief summary of what I have discovered. I hope, all the same, that it will give you an idea of the infinite potential of life 'in Christ'. In some Christian churches, alas, people hardly ever refer to the Holy Spirit; while in others, you hardly hear them talk of anything else, but sometimes quite distortedly, for they tend to limit His activities to one or two particular forms – and even these are often a misinterpretation of Scripture! Both these attitudes are mistaken, and equally tragic.

As the white light of the sun, when diffused, reveals a whole *spectrum* of seven colours, so the Holy Spirit, when He fills us, manifests Christ in our lives through a *sevenfold operation* that contains as great a wealth of variety as we perceive in nature itself, which is likewise His handiwork. Men offend and dishonour the Spirit of God by their tendency to reduce Him to a mere 'formula'. He is God. The cosmos itself cannot express all the beauty and complexity of His being.

The seven aspects of the Spirit's fullness

1. *The witness of the Spirit*
   (a) His very first act is *to witness to our spirit* that we are

(12) Jn. 13:34–35
(13) Acts 4:32–33

children of God.[14] 'He who believes on the Son of God has
this witness *in himself*.'[15] This is the very source of our
assurance. But we need to remember that *His witness is based
on the Word of God*, which He has created with this precise
end in view. The Spirit, the Word, and the Son of God are
inseparable. You must not and cannot dissociate them.
The Bible is the Spirit's handbook. You can't have Christ
without the Spirit, nor the Spirit without the Scriptures.

(b) Then He witnesses of Christ *through us*.[16] He backs up
our witness with divine authority, and this is the only way
we can convince men of the truth.

2. *The fruit of the Spirit*

He creates the fruit of the Spirit in us.[17] *This fruit is the
character of Jesus*, summarised in these nine words: 'Love,
joy, peace, patience, kindness, goodness, faithfulness,
gentleness, self-control'. These qualities are in fact the
multiple facets of *love*. A man is not filled with the Spirit of
God, whatever his claims, if he is not filled with the love of
Jesus – that is, if he is not prepared to be crucified for his
brother. Nor is he filled with the Spirit unless he is as humble
as a little child.[18]

When we are filled with the Holy Spirit, *we do love God*
with all our heart;[19] *we also love our neighbours* as ourselves;[20]
and *we love our brother* as Christ loved us.[21] It is a miracle,
but it is a fact.

3. *The communion of the Spirit*

He creates communion, or *fellowship*.[22] The Greek word
in the original means 'sharing'.

(a) When He fills us, the Spirit first brings us into extraordinary fellowship *with God*. We share everything with

(14) Rom. 8:16
(15) 1 Jn. 5:10
(16) Jn. 15:26–27
(17) Gal. 5:22
(18) Mt. 18:5
(19) Mt. 22:37
(20) Mt. 22:39
(21) Jn. 15:12
(22) 2 Cor. 13:13

Him[23] He is mine and I am His. We have in common everything that Christ is. I share with God the Object of His love.

(b) He then brings us into a deep fellowship *with our brothers*.[24] We share the life of Christ together, as in Acts 4:32. *The Spirit of God never divides believers;* He doesn't drive God's children apart. He unites them. You can be sure that anything that tears the body of Christ apart comes, not from God, but from an evil source.

4. The intercession of the Spirit

(a) *He intercedes.* He prays *for us* with 'sighs too deep for words'.[25] He is our second 'Advocate', our 'Barrister'.[26] This is the meaning of the Greek word translated 'Comforter' and 'Counsellor' in some versions of John 14. It is the same word as in 1 John 2:1, where Jesus is also called our 'Advocate'. Thus we have an Advocate in heaven at the right hand of God, and we also have an Advocate right beside us here on earth! What a potent backing!

(b) Then he prays *through us*.[27] The fullness of the Spirit finds expression in a life of intense prayer, for we ourselves become intercessors before God, as we pray in the 'holiest' on behalf of those without.

5. The teaching of the Spirit

(a) *He teaches us*.[28] The object of all his teaching is *to reveal the Lord Jesus Christ*, because it is only through Him that we can know the Father, and none but the Spirit of God can reveal the Son of God.

(b) *He uses the Word of God* to do this; the Bible becomes for us a book of crystal clarity, a mirror in which we discover the face of God.[29]

6. The guidance of the Spirit

He leads or guides us.[30] As Israel was led through the

(23) 1 Jn. 1:7
(24) 1 Jn. 1:3
(25) Rom. 8:26–27
(26) Jn. 14:16
(27) Jude v. 20
(28) 1 Jn. 2:20, 27; Jn. 16:13–15
(29) 2 Cor. 3:18; Ps. 119:130
(30) Rom. 8:14

desert by the Cloud of the presence of God, so, as the Spirit of God fills us, we become sensitive to His movements and He is thus able to guide us through the very desert itself into the fulfilment of God's promises in Christ for us. There are three means He uses in order to guide us:

(a) *The Scriptures.* If God clearly says a certain thing in the Bible, that is enough; we do not have to search for further guidance.

(b) *Circumstances.* When it comes to details, God frequently uses circumstances to point out His will in a particular situation. This is true for the believer who is walking close to God. As Hudson Taylor said, 'God becomes that man's one great Circumstance'.

(c) *The voice of God* in our conscience, an *inward conviction.* But such a conviction is never in conflict with the Scriptures; His voice does not contradict His Word. It is the Scriptures that enable us to 'discern the spirits' and expose Satan's trickeries when he tries to mimic the voice of God.

You will see that in Acts 10 God uses all these three means to direct Peter to Cornelius' house. What a blessing resulted for the world from that case of guidance! In the same way, in Genesis 24, the Spirit of God guided Abraham's servant, enabling him to find the woman who was to be the mother of the holy nation.

7. The gifts of the Spirit

He enables us to serve God effectively by means of spiritual gifts. The Holy Spirit's supreme desire is to make Christ known to the whole world, and, with this in view, He works to reveal Him to other people through us. He alone knows the best way for each one to serve God. God does not mass-produce men. You, as a soul, are utterly unique; God has created you specifically for Himself. His Spirit has a unique treasure of grace to give you, which only He can impart.

None of us can serve God merely with his human abilities. The 'flesh' cannot do the will of God; the one thing it *can* do is mess everything up! Even Moses had to spend forty years of humiliation in the desert to learn that hard truth; but when, after his encounter with God, he came back to face the terrible dictator of that time, with nothing but an old stick in his hand and the Word of God in his heart, what an outcome! Even this book you are reading now is a result of that impact!

So, my brother, ask God to endow you with those spiritual qualities you need in order to serve Him effectively.[31]

'Do not be drunk with wine . . . but be filled with the spirit[32]

This supremely important commandment is worth analysing very carefully.

Why is it men are always looking for stimulation through alcohol, drugs and all that sort of thing? It is simply because they lack the true stimulus of the Holy Spirit. This world's artificial stimulants leave us in a worse state than before. The only stimulant that can enable a man to do the will of God, and at the same time renew his powers and clarify his vision, is the Spirit of God. Even in the Christian world, there is a definite tendency to fall back on substitute 'stimulants' instead of relying on the Spirit of God. People like to depend on money, or a powerful organisation, or on some particular experience, or on some great man, rather than on God. Anything other than God leaves us desperate and baffled in the end.

All the same, the believer *does* need a stimulant. In time of war, the wretched soldier often gets a tot of rum to steel him to do the job he couldn't face in cold blood. The Christian likewise has to face a world that crucified his Master, and for this he needs supernatural courage and joy – and the Holy Spirit does give us astonishing courage and an overflowing joy.

The clue to the true meaning

Now let us look more closely at this verse. The full meaning of the original is not usually brought out in translation. The Greek verb here is in the *continuous imperative* tense. The sentence is best translated: '*Keep getting filled* with the Spirit.' So it is a continuous, ceaseless action, not a single, final, once-for-all experience. In Greek there is indeed a 'simple' or 'definite' imperative, but Paul does not use it in

(31) See chapter 10 for a rather more detailed study of 'spiritual gifts'.
(32) Eph. 5:18

this context; he deliberately uses the continuous form of the verb.

This is most significant. The Holy Spirit thus reveals to us a very important truth about Himself. *We do not receive the fullness of the Holy Spirit once for all!* It is not a 'final' experience. Nobody can claim that he has 'got it for good'.

The new birth, on the other hand, is an irreversible act of God; if I am a child of God now, I shall always be so. I cannot be the child of my parents today, something else tomorrow, and then, the following day, once again my parents' child. Thank God for the certainty of the new birth! Whereas the fact that I am filled with the Spirit of God today does not in any way guarantee that I shall be filled tomorrow. We can at any time lose the fullness of the Spirit; and yet, thank God, we can also recover it, though there is often quite a price to pay.[33]

You aren't a bottle!

Lots of people think you can obtain the fullness of the Spirit in the same way as you fill a bottle with champagne! You can then carefully cork it up, stick an attractive label on yourself, and go around for the rest of your life, saying: 'I got it in such and such a year'! But what is the use of a bottle in your cellar, or even on the table, unless it is broken open and its contents are poured out?

No, it just isn't possible to have the fullness of the Holy Spirit like that. We cannot have God and keep Him simply for ourselves. Solomon was right when he said that the heaven and the heaven of heavens could not contain God[34] and a mere human being certainly can't! We can only experience the fullness of God in so far as we allow His Spirit *to pour through us*. The human soul is nothing like a bottle! It is more like a pipe or an electric wire; or, better still, we can say it resembles a mountain torrent or a river. A river, to be a river, must fulfil two conditions: it must receive its water ceaselessly from the highland springs and at the same time give it out continuously into the valley below. We, in the same way, can only be filled with the

(33) See chapters 5, 6, 7
(34) 2 Chr. 6:18. See also Is. 40:12–28

Spirit of God as we receive this fullness direct from on high, *moment by moment*, and as we communicate it, giving it out to the world around us. God intends us to be a river, not a pond! A canal, not a bottle!

The real meaning of the Spirit's fullness

In other words, we cannot obtain the fullness of the Spirit merely for our own personal satisfaction. It is given *to enable us to do the will of God*. Man's only real satisfaction comes from doing the will of God. When God finds a man who loves Him enough to live for Him, He opens His heart to him and makes him the vehicle of His love. All the energy and intelligence and generosity of God are available to that man for the supreme purpose of doing God's will – and that means *making Christ known to the world*.

Just as a tree, obeying the laws of nature, is both a source of value to the earth and also a thing of beauty that satisfies the human spirit, so the man who lives according to the laws of God finds a deep satisfaction for himself, while at the same time he becomes what Jesus calls 'the light of the world' and 'the salt of the earth'.[35] The greatest satisfaction a child of God can know is to be able to lead another soul to God. God Himself becomes the satisfaction of such a man.

God is love, and the Bible says that man is made in the image of God. Man therefore reaches the summit of his experience when he loves; or, rather, when the Spirit of God begins to love through him. Without God, man's heart is empty; and the pain of his empty heart drives him everywhere looking for a purpose in life. But when God fills this void, man discovers the true reason for his own being in Him who is its Source. His life has taken on significance. His personality becomes radiant, transformed by the Spirit of God. He discovers love.

Why those two lakes?

The Holy Land itself offers us a marvellous illustration of the principle of spiritual fullness. It contains two great lakes: the Lake of Galilee and the Dead Sea; and these yield a

(35) Mt. 5:13

striking spiritual symbolism. The two lakes receive the same water, which flows down from Hermon, the highest mountain in the country; and yet they are as different as life and death.

The Lake of Galilee, lying close to the snows of Hermon, receives its water straight from the source, and gives out all that it receives. This living water streams unceasingly through the lake and flows on out down the lower Jordan valley. It is fresh and full of fish, and it sustains an abundant life along its shores, where Jesus Himself once lived.

The Dead Sea, on the other hand, receives the very same water, but it does not draw it from the source itself; it receives it 'second hand', through the Lake of Galilee. It does not give out anything it receives. It is situated in a deep hollow, at such a low level – 1300 feet below the level of the Mediterranean – that the heat is suffocating. It loses in evaporation all the water it receives; all that is left is a bitterness that intensifies year by year and makes life impossible either in the lake or on its shores. Everything is dried up, sterile, salt-ridden, sheer desert. They say that even a bird flying over this sea falls asphyxiated; a single drop of this water in the eye galls like an acid. I know, because I have felt it.

The meaning of this symbolism

Now let us learn the truth that the finger of God has written into the configuration of the Holy Land.

The spiritual believer is like the Lake of Galilee. He lives near to God, close to the Source of his being. He is constantly revived by an endless stream of divine life pouring through him. Because he is at all times open both to God and to men, the Spirit of God fills him and constantly renews the life of Christ in and around him.

The carnal believer is like the Dead Sea. He is a long way from the Source; he depends on other Christians for his spiritual life, instead of finding his resources in direct and deep fellowship with God. He does indeed receive the Spirit of God in good measure, but he is incapable of retaining or using this wealth. He lives on such a low spiritual level that the abundance escapes him as soon as he receives it. His soul is continually disappointed; he experiences a bitterness that grows more acute each year. He is incapable of communicating or sustaining spiritual life around him. It is true, thank

God, that the waters of the Dead Sea will one day be healed.[36]
So also there is hope for the carnal Christian; but only if he
allows God to intervene.

God intends the fullness of the Spirit to be the normal state
of every single disciple of Christ. But what a tragedy as we
look at the actual situation around us! We have to admit that
abnormal Christians are terribly plentiful on this earth.
Surely, my brother, you are not going to swell their number!
No, on the contrary, 'keep getting filled' with the Spirit all the
time, from this very day on!

Are you a Lake of Galilee? Or a Dead Sea?

(36) Ezek. 47:8–9

Part II

THE THREE SPIRITUAL PRINCIPLES

PROLOGUE

The Seven Pillars of Wisdom

'No one can lay any foundation other than the one already laid, which is Jesus Christ.'[1]

'Wisdom has built her house: she has set up her seven pillars.'[2]

The wisdom of God is teaching you to build your spiritual life. The foundation was laid when you were born again, and, ever since, the temple has been under construction. If it is built according to the principles of divine wisdom, the edifice will resist every storm and shock.[3] The Christian is free to build, on the foundation of his faith, either with perishable materials resembling wood, hay or stubble, none of which can withstand fire or tempest; or else with lasting materials resembling gold, silver and valuable stone that nothing can destroy.[4] At the return of Christ, when we meet God face to face, the building will either stand firm or collapse. The foundation will remain – our faith in Christ is not taken away from us; but the structure we have built upon it may disappear like smoke. In that case, we shall lose, not our salvation, but our 'reward'.[5]

What are the Seven Pillars of Wisdom, on which the House of God rests? As a young man, I was impressed by this passage of Scripture. I was convinced there must be seven basic principles, seven fundamental truths, upon which God builds our spiritual life into a firm reality. It took me many years to grasp the seven truths I am setting out in the following chapters.

(1) 1 Cor. 3:11 (New International Version)
(2) Prov. 9:1
(3) Mt. 7:25
(4) 1 Cor. 3:12–15
(5) Verse 15

Three principles and four disciplines

As I went through the whole Bible year after year, I found
three basic spiritual *principles* without which the life of
fullness cannot exist, and also four *disciplines* or habits we
need to develop in order to nourish and strengthen that life.
You can think of it all, if you like, as a table composed of
three boards and supported by four legs. In the following
chapters we shall be examining, first, the three principles,
and after that, the four disciplines.

Perhaps you think I am rather complicating things. Not in
the least! As the seven colours of the rainbow fuse into a
single white light, so all these spiritual factors add up to a
single condition for obtaining God's grace, and that is *faith* –
faith in *Christ*. Faith is the one and only condition for
salvation: in the New Testament there are about a hundred
and fifty passages that state this clearly. How often Jesus
used to say: 'Be it according to your faith'!

The apostle Paul, in his epistles, insists that, *having begun
by faith, we have to go on by faith*. We cannot possibly achieve
perfection by our own efforts. It is God who begins, and it is
God who completes.

Only the Spirit of God can give us eternal life; only the
Spirit of God can develop that life. The secret of life in Christ
consists in only one thing: faith in Christ. In the following
chapters, as I define these 'Seven Pillars', I really have only a
single thought: the need to believe in Christ for absolutely
everything. Not only for the world to come, but also for the
things that belong to our present existence here on earth.

There are three 'stages' in salvation – past, present, and
future; but, according to the Bible, faith is the one key to
them all. It is by faith in Christ that you were saved from the
punishment of your sin; it is by faith also that, at His return,
you will be saved from the very *presence* of sin; and so,
likewise, it is by faith that you are saved day by day from the
power of sin.

However, the Bible reveals that there are *two obstacles* to
faith: an evil conscience and an evil will. We are now going
to examine these two problems.

The basis of our study

If you begin to study under a famous professor, he will

expect you to get a copy of the book or books he has written and work through them carefully. We Christians have a divine 'professor': our Teacher is the Spirit of truth, and He has written a comprehensive textbook known as the Bible! It is utter folly to suppose we can really benefit from His tuition unless we are prepared to make a deep study of His *written* work.

Only four commandments

The Holy Spirit tells us a great deal about Himself in the Bible, but gives us *only four commandments* referring to Himself. By these four He sums up the terms of the relationship He wishes to establish between us and Himself. It is therefore supremely important that we grasp the meaning of these four commandments and begin to live by them. We have already studied the first of these in the preceding chapter. I call it the *general* commandment: 'Keep getting filled with the Spirit.' But this does not tell us exactly *how* to 'keep getting filled'.

The three spiritual principles

The three other commandments do answer this question, and for this reason I call them the three *specific* commandments. They are the three basic principles of the spiritual life, the three essential conditions for the fullness of the Holy Spirit, which appear and reappear all through Scripture.[6] Two of these commandments are negative and concern your conscience and your will. The third is positive and concerns your faith.

If we can understand the meaning of these three commandments or principles, and, with God's help, put them into practice, we have every reason to believe that God will fill us with His Spirit. The three following chapters are given over to the study of these *three principles*, the conditions on which the fullness of the Spirit depends.

After that we will go on to study what I call the *four disciplines*,[7] by means of which these three spiritual principles

(6) For example, in 1 Tim. 1:5 and Heb. 10:22. Also, in the Levitical offerings in Lev. chapters 1–5.

(7) The four 'commandments' concerning the Holy Spirit must not be confused with the four 'disciplines'!

are strengthened and supported. The Wisdom of God can thus build your spiritual life into a structure of lasting value, on the basis of these seven divinely-conceived 'Pillars'. I have never found any other spiritual factors of comparable importance.

5

THE PROBLEM OF YOUR CONSCIENCE

The first spiritual principal:
'Do not grieve the Holy Spirit of God.' [1]

What do you do when, in spite of the fact that you are now born again, you find you have done something wrong?

The Scriptures tell us that nothing can separate us from the love of God; [2] but our conscience seems to tell us the very opposite. When we have disobeyed God, we feel that we have lost His approval. We dare not face Him any more; we no longer feel able to pray or to speak of Him to others. In other words, we have a bad conscience.

We find ourselves in an agonising dilemma. On the one hand, the Bible tells us that God has blotted out our sins and considers us righteous as Christ is righteous; on the other hand, we ourselves feel really guilty. So what should our attitude be?

The reply is obvious: *we must repent*. But what then? Do we need to obtain God's forgiveness all over again?

Our accuser and our advocate

The Scriptures reveal that, in heaven itself, we have both an accuser and an Advocate. According to Revelation 12:10, the devil is 'the *accuser* of the brethren, who accuses them day and night before God'. While in 1 John 2:1 we read: 'I am writing this to you so that you do not sin; but, if any one does sin, we have an *Advocate* with the Father, Jesus Christ the righteous.'

When you sin it is not the Lord Jesus who is accusing you; it is the devil. The devil puts pressure on your conscience, which, of course, recognises the evil you have done; but he wants to make you believe it is God who is condemning you,

(1) Eph. 4:30
(2) Rom. 8:31–39

and that He has shut the door against you. His whole object is so to distort the image of God in your thinking that you forget the value of the blood of Christ. Instead of seeing God in Christ crucified, reconciling you to Himself, he wants you to see Him as an enemy, as though Christ has a grudge against you, rejecting you, loving you no longer. It is more difficult to believe in the love of God than in anything else; and, if the devil succeeds in stripping you of the certainty of this, he can then plunge you into discouragement and despair. That is the way the accuser gets the better of you.

Of course, he would be absolutely right if Jesus hadn't died to efface this very sin and risen again to prove your acquittal. Satan has a terrible weapon in the shape of God's righteousness and law. But it is now a *false* argument, because God's righteousness and law are already satisfied.

You can look upon it this way: the devil stands at God's left hand to accuse you; your conscience feels all the weight of his accusation, but he tries to make you believe that it is the righteousness of God that is condemning you: this is why you feel crushed and beaten. But look again! At God's right hand you have an Advocate for your defence, answering for all your failures. Jesus isn't accusing you! He is pleading your cause; He is praying, interceding for you. This is the theme of that marvellous Epistle to the Hebrews.[3] The Father looks upon the pierced hands of His Son. Before His face is the eternal argument of that precious blood poured out for you, an argument that shuts the accuser's mouth. To the devil's accusation, Jesus replies: 'The righteousness of the law of God is now utterly satisfied because this sin is already wiped out. The cross is a finished work. I have paid in person for this offence. I have already suffered the hell this man deserved. He is free.' My brother, my sister, the scars in Jesus' hands, the blood which He shed, are the everlasting witness that your case is closed. The records are filed away. There is no more to be said.

Satan is strong and crafty; if you listen to his accusations, you will be in a state of perpetual discouragement, tormented by your conscience. You will end by forgetting what Christ has done for you. But if you listen to the voice of your

(3) As you will discover in the following passages: Heb. 2:17–18; 4:14–16; 7:11–15, 24–28; 9:11–15, 24; 10:10–14, 19–22.

Advocate, you will hear every time these marvellous words: 'You are forgiven. Your sin is wiped out.' That is the miracle of the grace of God. Christ's work on the cross was not only to save you from a future hell, but to save you today from the accuser. You are forgiven.

Too easy?

Somebody is sure to answer me: 'All that is very beautiful, but it is much too easy! What? You mean I can sin against God, and then, without doing anything further about it, I find every time the record is wiped clean! *My* conscience does not let me believe in such an easy way out!'

Oh! You are dead right not to believe in an easy solution! For God the 'way out' wasn't easy! Your very least failure cost God the torture and death of His Son. The blood of Jesus was anything but an 'easy solution'. But God wants you to believe in the absolute value of that unique sacrifice. Jesus Himself cried out on the cross: 'It is finished.'[4] Not to count on His forgiveness is, in fact, unbelief. The devil's very objective is to rob you of this certainty and plunge you back into torment. In this way he paralyses your spiritual life, he keeps your faith impotent.

But, 'if God is for us, who can be against us? Who shall bring any charge against God's elect? [Do you think God will?] It is God who justifies! Who will condemn them? [Will Christ?] It is Christ who died, yes, rather was raised from the dead, who is at the right hand of God, who *intercedes* for us! . . . Who will be able to separate us from the love of God in Christ?'[5]

Too easy? The fact is, *there is no other way* of obtaining God's forgiveness. Thank God for it, and take it.

Do you realise the completeness of the work God has done for you? Have you really understood the worth of the blood of Christ? God calls us to come into His presence *because Jesus is our Priest, our 'Barrister', and not our enemy.*[6]

But, you say, is this knowledge really all we need in order to regain our fellowship with God?

(4) Jn. 19:30
(5) Rom. 8:31–35
(6) Heb. 10:19–22

The two aspects of God's forgiveness

Well, there is one condition for the liberation of our conscience. The New Testament shows us very clearly that the only basis for God's pardon is the blood of Jesus; but there are two aspects of this forgiveness:

God's judicial forgiveness

Before I was born again, God was my Judge, and I was the murderer of His Son, pursued by His law. But on that day God, as Judge, forgave all my sin, past, present, and future. Ever since that moment, God no longer sees my sin; in His eyes I am righteous as Jesus is righteous. He considers that my sin now 'belongs' to Jesus and that, as His death is mine, the sin problem is solved: His death cancels out my sin. The righteousness of Jesus has become my righteousness. My heart now belongs to Jesus and His resurrection has become my new life. By that act of God which Paul, in Romans 6:3–4, calls spiritual baptism (of which water baptism is the picture or symbol), I have been identified with Jesus Christ in his death and in his resurrection. Since He now reckons me dead and buried with Christ, He can at last forgive me, which He could not do before; and it is thanks to His forgiveness that I can now receive His life of resurrection; it is given to me the moment His Spirit enters into me.[7] Thus, the new birth is the direct result of God's judicial pardon, and this pardon is final.[8] It is a good thing our salvation depends upon an act of God and not upon steadfastness.

God's fatherly forgiveness

From the moment of my new birth, God is no longer my Judge; He has become my Father. I am no longer a criminal in His eyes; I have become His child. I call Him Father, 'Abba' or 'Daddy'.[9] When I am conscious of having sinned, He doesn't deal with me any longer in a court of law, but as a Father face to face with His child. God, as Judge, no longer sees my sin; but to my conscience it is real enough, and I find this unendurable. A great, black cloud has come between me and the light of His presence. I am still His child and He is

(7) Ezek. 37:10, 14
(8) Heb. 10:17, 18
(9) Rom. 8:15

still my Father; but I no longer see His face. I have lost, not my salvation, but my intimacy or my fellowship with Him.

It was to illustrate this truth that Jesus told the story of the prodigal son.[10] The son was still the son of his father, but he was in a state of rebellion, away from home, and leading a wretched life among the pigs. He was afraid to return to his father; there is no doubt that he had a false idea of his father's character. He expected to be met in righteous anger, whip in hand, with the dogs snarling. Yet it was the very opposite that happened. For, when in the end he did return, confessing his sin and asking for forgiveness, he found his father longing for him; he was kissed and reinstated in the family. The father even gave him of his best.

So Jesus teaches me *to return* to my heavenly Father after every failure and *to confess* my fault honestly to Him. Satan will do all he can to stop me; he will try to convince me that my Father will drive me away from His presence, and that He would rather I stayed away, far away, among the pigs. As long as I don't believe in God's forgiveness, Satan keeps me in a state of spiritual depression and weakness. For, while my conscience is thus soiled, *the Holy Spirit is grieved and ceases to fill me*. This is Satan's objective.

To obtain God's *judicial* forgiveness, there is, as we have said, only one condition, repeated over and over again in the New Testament. Such a passage is Acts 16:31, which says: '*Believe* on the Lord Jesus and you will be saved.'

In the same way, to obtain God's *fatherly* forgiveness, there is just one condition: 'If we *confess* our sins, God is faithful and just to forgive them and to cleanse us from all unrighteousness.'[11] Note that this passage, like the whole of John's first Epistle, is meant for believers.

Yes, just as we have obtained God's judicial pardon simply by faith in Christ, so also we obtain His fatherly forgiveness simply by faith in Christ, on the basis of Christ's sacrifice, a sacrifice that was made once for all.[12] What God requires of us now is truth, absolute honesty. He demands a straight confession. He insists that we must admit what we have done. What He will not tolerate is our trying to justify

(10) Lk. ch. 15
(11) 1 Jn. 1:9
(12) Heb. 9:12, 26–27; 10:10, 12, 14, 18

or excuse ourselves, or our evading the issue. We have to call sin by its true name: sin. At that very moment we receive God's fatherly forgiveness. We already have His judicial forgiveness; but now He pardons us also as Father – but still and ever for the same reason: the blood of His Son was shed for our sin. He is 'faithful' to forgive (for He has promised it), and He is just or 'righteous' to forgive (for Christ died and rose again). So He pardons us *and also purifies us* from all sin – if we confess it.

So the condition, the only one, for obtaining the forgiveness of our heavenly Father, is our confession of the sin in question. We can do nothing about atoning for it. We are not even expected to, since Christ has already done that. We are simply required to present ourselves before Him just as we are, like the leper in Matthew 8:2, whom Jesus cured instantly. 'God is light.'[13] In the light of His face, every imperfection is immediately laid bare. 'If we walk in the light, we have fellowship one with another and the blood of His Son cleanses us from all sin.'[14]

To my confession, God replies: 'My child, the matter was settled two thousand years ago by my Son on the cross; we needn't discuss it any more.' He turns the page of my record over; He never brings the matter up again. Nevertheless, He faces me again with the cross. It is an empty cross, but I hear my Father's voice saying to me: 'My child, remember the blood of My Son! That is the price of your pardon and the reason why you are once again in fellowship with Me.'

Through this discipline, I am able to rise again purified after every failure, but also with an increased hatred of sin. More than ever I understand God's love for me, His incredible generosity, His astonishing forgiveness of my wretched self, and the appalling nature of sin.

To whom should we confess our sin?

The Bible teaches that all known sin should be confessed to God, since all sin is a violation of His law. Thus, the Apostle Paul could say: 'I have lived before God in all good conscience up to this day.'[15] He did not mean that he had

(13) 1 Jn. 1:5
(14) 1 Jn. 1:7
(15) Acts 23:1

never sinned since his conversion, but rather that he had always made a point of confessing his sin; he had each time squared his accounts with God.

But if my sin concerns also my neighbour, if I have wronged my brother, it is not enough to confess it to God alone. It is necessary to confess to God first, that goes without saying; but God will reply to me: 'My child, I am not the only one concerned in this matter, you have also sinned against your brother. Go to him and confess your sin, then come to me and I will pardon you. If your brother forgives you, so much the better; if he doesn't forgive you, at least you have cleared your conscience. You must be honest, not only with Me, but also with men.'

If I have committed a sin which becomes public and drags the name of Christ in the dirt, then God expects a public confession also. There again, He insists that I should be honest, that I acknowledge the truth, that I walk in the light. God demands that His Son's name be honoured.

Listen again to Paul: 'I always take pains', he said, 'to have a clear conscience toward God *and toward men.*'[16]

Don't we need a 'Confessor'?

If my sin is an offence against God alone, it is to Him alone that I ought to confess it. The Scriptures nowhere teach the necessity of confessing to anyone except the person whom we have offended. If a human being begins to receive everybody else's confessions, how can he remain pure and upright in his own soul? Man is not fitted for that. It is God's work.

It is true that, at times, we need to ask counsel of a man of God or of a friend, and to open our hearts to him; there are some burdens that we simply cannot carry alone. But we should be careful in doing this; we need to consider the conscience of the one to whom we unburden ourselves. He also is a mere human and a sinner. He also has need of our prayers. We have no right to make him a spiritual dustbin!

'Do not grieve the Holy Spirit of God.' [17]

This, then, is the second commandment which the Spirit

(16) Acts 24:16
(17) Eph. 4:30

of God gives us about Himself; it is the first of the three *specific* commandments, the first *condition* for living in His fullness.

What is it that grieves Him? Why, our sin, of course! Yet grieving Him is *worse still* than sinning. *It is remaining in a state of sin.* It is retaining a bad or evil conscience. This is serious, for when the Spirit is grieved, He ceases to fill us. We are left to flounder in our own strength until we learn by bitter experience that we cannot afford to neglect the voice of that 'holy Angel in Whom is God's name' and Who was sent to guide us into the promised blessing.[18] When we grieve Him, He is still there; but, instead of filling our house, He withdraws into the attic or is driven into the cellar.

It is dangerous to grieve the Spirit of God. We read in Isaiah 63:10 that Israel, in the wilderness, grieved the Holy Spirit with the result that He became their enemy and fought against them! He was still in the midst of the camp; the glory of God was in the tabernacle; but He refused to lead them any longer. They lost thirty-eight precious years, tramping disconsolately about in the desert.

But immediately I confess my sin I cease to grieve the Holy Spirit, and once again He fills me. I am back in fellowship with my Father. He doesn't mind how much I weep over my sin, so long as I am in His arms and not in the far country among the pigs.

This first condition of the fullness of the Spirit can be summed up therefore in a single word: *repentance*. But repentance is not simply sorrow. The prodigal son was very sad indeed among the swine, but that did him no good! He had to admit the truth and *confess* his sin to the Father whom he had offended. True repentance always expresses itself in confession of sin: otherwise it is futile, like the remorse of Esau, who was rejected, despite his tears.[19]

'*He who conceals his transgressions will not prosper, but he who confesses and forsakes them will obtain mercy.*'[20]

(18) Ex. 23:20–22
(19) Heb. 12:17
(20) Prov. 28:13

6

THE PROBLEM OF YOUR WILL

*The second spiritual principle:
'Do not quench the Spirit.'*[1]

The second obstacle to faith is *an evil will*. Every single day, and many times a day, we need to examine our conscience and also our will, in order to be continually right with God. Otherwise, our faith declines.

This second principle, then, has to do with our *will*. It is the second specific commandment concerning the Holy Spirit. To quench the Spirit means to *resist* Him. When you quench or cover up a flame, it goes out; the embers are still there, but they are no longer aflame.

Disobedience quenches the Spirit

After tempting God ten times in the desert, Israel reached the point, not only of grieving, but also of quenching the Holy Spirit.[2] During all the thirty-eight long years that followed, even though He was in the camp, He remained silent. Whereas, before their rebellion, God had given them revelation upon revelation through Moses, afterwards He almost ceased to communicate with them. It was a time of painful sterility. Israel had disobeyed deliberately, and so the Spirit of God took them at their word and left them alone. It is a terrible punishment when the Holy Spirit no longer disturbs us or impels us, when He no longer opens up the heaven of fellowship with the Father.

That can happen, not only to individuals, but also to churches, communities, and spiritual movements. The history of Christianity is full of tragic examples of this. The Spirit of God is very patient, very compassionate; He does everything He can to bring us to obedience; but He does not

(1) 1 Thess. 5:19
(2) Num. 14:20–23

force us to obey. He respects our personality and our will – whereas the evil spirits respect neither. So that, if I persist in disobedience, the Holy Spirit ends up by taking me at my word; He says no more. That is the most devastating thing that can happen to a child of God or to a church.

Every act of disobedience is in fact the beginning of this process; every bit of self-will leads eventually to the quenching of the Spirit. The Bible insists from Genesis to Revelation on the need for obedience to the voice of God. If man does not obey the laws of nature, he inevitably suffers the consequences of his folly. The wise man conforms his life to the laws of physics, chemistry, and biology; he well knows that they exist to keep him alive and healthy, and that any abuse of them will result in the deterioration of his faculties or even death. So likewise, the spiritual Christian (that is, the intelligent one!), orders his life according to the laws of the Spirit of God, knowing that they are designed for his happiness, and that they bring him nearer to God. The Holy Spirit has inspired the whole of Scripture so that we may know God's thought and thus respect it. If in the physical realm disobedience is dangerous, how much more so is it in the spiritual realm!

The difference between obedience and legalism

The New Testament condemns legalism but insists on obedience. Moreover, it distinguishes between 'dead works'[3] and 'good works'.[4] *Dead* works are the efforts of the flesh to justify itself and pass itself off as something of value; their motive is pride or selfishness. *Good* works, on the other hand, are the spontaneous blossoming of the life of Christ in us. The legalist works with the idea of 'buying' God's favour, or of impressing other people; the spiritual believer, because he is already saved, acts out of love and gratitude to God.

There is really no conflict between faith and the law. Jesus, in Matthew 22:37–40, sums up the whole law of God in a single word: *love*. If I love God with all my heart, I shall spontaneously do the things that are pleasing to Him, and I shall turn in horror from those which He regards as sin. If I

(3) Heb. 6:1; 9:14
(4) 1 Tim. 5:10; 2 Tim. 3:14; Tit. 2:7; 3:1, 8, 14, etc.

love my neighbour as myself, I will not harm him for anything in the world; rather, I will do anything I can to help him.

Love is the fulfilling of the law

'The fruit of the Spirit is love.'[5] To be filled with the Spirit is to have a real and intense love for God and for my neighbour; it means being impelled by the constant desire to do the will of God and to do good to my neighbour. Thus Paul says that 'love is the fulfilling of the law',[6] and that true faith 'works by love'.[7] The fullness of the Spirit develops my faith, which in turn expresses itself in love; and love wants to act for the best. The law of God is *written in my heart* by the Spirit;[8] that law is no longer a galling yoke, but a sheer joy.

The night before He died, in that upper room, when His heart was no doubt breaking with anguish, Jesus said to His disciples: 'If you love Me, keep My commandments.'[9] It is our obedience to Christ that proves our love for Him.

Then, in the same passage,[10] the Lord Jesus promises, to those who do keep His commandments, a revelation of Himself and of His love beyond all imagination, to such a degree that the Father Himself manifests himself to them. The disobedient Christian knows nothing of these extraordinary blessings; he lives on the mere edge of reality, in the half-light of earth. On the other hand, the man who is living in open communion with God is already, in a sense, experiencing Heaven – since Heaven is the presence of Christ.

The joy of doing the impossible

But the will of God is often difficult to accomplish. God requires acts of courage and devotion of which we ourselves are incapable. I think that all true spiritual life (that which accomplishes the will of God) is in fact supernatural. Without the fullness of the Spirit, it is impossible to live the Christ-life in this world which crucified Him. Such a life is, however,

(5) Gal. 5:22
(6) Rom. 13:10
(7) Gal. 5:6
(8) Heb. 10:16
(9) Jn. 14:15
(10) Jn. 14:22–23

possible to the man who *believes*. Did not Jesus always say that we receive according to our faith?

The Apostle Paul calls this '*the obedience of faith*'.[11] The Bible is full of examples of this faith. Noah believed in God; that is why he built the ark[12] – what an act of faith and obedience! Abraham believed; that is why he 'went out', not knowing where he was going,[13] Moses dared to appear before Pharaoh, without any weapon or human power.[14] Joshua, faced with the Jordan in flood, obeyed God and marched with his people straight towards the water.[15] Likewise, at the command of Jesus, the handicapped man lifted his withered arm and was healed *as he obeyed*.[16]

We, as children of God, are expected to obey in the same way. Even when God's will appears to be impossible, so long as He calls or commands, we must obey Him. Oh, the reward will be great enough! The history of the true church and of Christ's great missionaries is a mass of examples, the stories of men and women of all sorts, mostly without any special natural abilities, but who counted on God for the impossible and achieved it.

The folly of a mere 90 per cent obedience

I think of the tragic story of King Saul.[17] Three times he disobeyed the Word of God, always on apparently unimportant issues. He did the will of God, but not completely. He compromised, and that is a grievous failing in a spiritual leader. God rejected him, and his shocking end is still a solemn warning to everybody.[18]

Why did God reject a man who had to a considerable extent done His will? The reason is that God is love, and love has to give all, but also claims all in return. No marriage can last if it isn't built on a foundation of reciprocal and whole-hearted love. Love cannot tolerate any infidelity. Because

(11) Rom. 1:5
(12) Heb. 11:7
(13) Heb. 11:8; Rom. 4:18–21
(14) Heb. 11:24–27
(15) Josh. 3:5–17; 4:10, 18
(16) Mt. 12:13
(17) 1 Sam. chapters. 13–15
(18) 1 Sam. chapters. 28–31

God loves with an absolute love, the depth of which can only be measured by the cross, He cannot tolerate a half-hearted love from us. No girl would ever give herself in marriage to a boy who promised her only 90 per cent of his life and heart – unless she were crazy!

In that ineffable dialogue that God is seeking to create between Himself and your soul, He longs for an unreserved interchange and openness. There is a verse in the book of Proverbs where God says: 'My son, give me your heart!'[19] That is the obedience which God seeks.

To the man who gives Him his heart, God opens His very heaven. He begins to give Himself and to unveil His love. He brings His vast resources within human reach. This is what He calls the *fullness* of His Spirit. The man who is always 'calculating' will never possess this treasure: love does not allow such holding back. You need to come back to the cross every single day to learn this afresh.

So the second condition for the fullness of the Spirit can likewise be summed up in one word: *obedience*. Most of all, obedience to the Word of God.

(19) Prov. 23:26

7

ADVANCE!

*The third spiritual principle:
'Walk by the Spirit.'* [1]

The third principle of the spiritual life (which is also the fourth, and last, commandment concerning the Holy Spirit) can also be summed up in a single word: *faith*. 'Walk by the Spirit' means: 'Believe in Christ'!

Advance by the Spirit

To 'walk' means to get moving! We have to forge ahead; it is fatal to remain stationary. The world in which we live is like an escalator – going down. It is a streaming river, carrying us away. We have to forge our way upwards, we have to travel against the current – and that means moving faster than the downward trend!

That's difficult, you say! Yes, it *is* difficult. Without the intervention of God's Spirit, it is really impossible. 'Walking by the Spirit' means advancing, pressing forward in the face of sheer impossibilities, even in the face of death. We are not expected to achieve this of our own ability, but with the power that comes from God. Remember how, in front of the Red Sea, God told His people to *go forward*. It was *as they prepared to obey* that God drove the sea back.[2] Christ told the paralysed man to get up and he was healed *as he acted*.[3]

To 'walk by the Spirit' means *to do the will of God*. This always seems virtually impossible to us. In fact, everything in the spiritual life is really beyond mere human capacity. Who indeed can live the life of Jesus? Yet God orders us

(1) Gal. 5:16
(2) Ex. 14:15
(3) Mk. 2:11–12

to advance – like Peter, when he got out of the boat to walk on the water to Jesus. We obey, we push ahead by faith; then God acts and achieves His purpose. We constantly find ourselves faced with huge difficulties; we cannot, on our own, do what God wants; but we obey, relying on His Spirit. Our faith is involved to the utmost; the very promises of God are at stake. We are compelled either to believe in Christ or to collapse in unbelief.

But God never lets us down! He never disappoints the man who really obeys Him and puts his trust in Him. Of course, He tests our faith – to the very limit. At times, we feel we can't stand any more; but God doesn't let us sink. We have to learn to endure suffering; Jesus never promised an easy life to His disciples; to follow Him means accepting the cross in our lives. But then we experience, every single time, the meaning of His resurrection. To walk by the Spirit means to accept what God says, that we are dead with Christ, that we are no longer seeking our own way – but it also means entering into the power of His resurrection.

Why does God say 'Walk'?

In the Apostle Paul's time, the only way to travel from one town to another, was to walk, or else to be carried or drawn by a walking animal! You could only move one step at a time. And, of course, in the spiritual life, there is no way of going forward except by walking. We don't as yet possess spiritual Rolls-Royces or celestial jet-planes! If we want to advance spiritually, we have to walk; and that means, we can only take one step at a time.

Our spiritual life begins with an *act* of faith, which then involves us in an *attitude* of faith; this attitude leads us subsequently to many *fresh acts* of faith; our spiritual life becomes in fact a succession of acts of faith. We live in constant dependence on God. Having begun by faith, we have to go on by faith.[4]

It is simply not possible to take two such steps at once, nor to take the third or the tenth step before the first. If I don't obey God today, in the first, immediate task which He tells me to carry out, I shall never progress to do His will

(4) Gal. 3:2–3; 5:25

on a larger scale. If, says Christ, I am not faithful now in little things, who will entrust me with the true riches?[5]

It is important to note the Greek verb in this commandment. It is in the continuous imperative tense. '*Keep on walking*'. Advance, push ahead all the time, without stopping, every day, moment by moment. A never-ceasing faith in Christ. No Christian can afford to say, 'I've got there' however far he has got! There is always new territory to win and explore.

We walk by faith and not by sight[6]

At every moment of such a life, your faith is being put to the test. If you believe in Christ, you will obey Him. If you go forward relying on Him, He will accomplish His will in you. Each step taken prepares you for the next stage. This is the way God deepens your faith; this is the way you grow.

Ah! You would so much like to know in advance where the road leads! But if that were the case, there would no longer be any need for faith. On the contrary, what God most wants is your trusting confidence; He asks you to put your trust in Him at every step. This is only reasonable, for in fact we depend utterly upon Him for our very existence.

Faith and reason

God never does violence to man's reason. True, He demands that we follow Him by faith and not by reason; but He always takes our reason into account. Evil spirits, on the contrary when they possess a man, obliterate his personality, his reason, and his will. The Spirit of God never does that; He respects our humanity. But He knows that our reason, damaged by sin and often baffled by the countless voices and influences that crowd in from outside, is incapable, without the guidance of His Spirit, of finding its way through the invisible world.

Faith, on the other hand, is that faculty of spiritual perception or discernment which is given us at the new birth. *It is never in conflict with reason.* By means of faith, God brings within the reach of our reason the truths which

(5) Lk. 16:11
(6) 2 Cor. 5:7

reason then recognises as authentic and which satisfy it. Faith is the spiritual 'sense' which enables us to see and touch and understand God. By means of this 'sense', or 'perception', our reason or mind is enlightened and thus enabled to make true decisions. Without faith, reason is restricted, limited by a 'ceiling' of spiritual insensitivity or unconsciousness; it has to work in the dark. That explains the failure of all non-Biblical philosophy. Faith and reason, on the other hand, walk hand in hand and in step with each other, with faith always one step ahead! Yet reason is always justified by the outcome.

Faith is not blind, as some people think. False faith is blind, of course; that is fanaticism. But true faith, based on divine revelation, sees its objective very clearly, and a long way ahead. God does not ask us to believe against all evidence, as human creeds do; at each step He gives us just enough light to enable us to be sure of the right way.

There is nothing illogical about that. When you fall in love, it isn't your reason that dictates whom you are to love; nevertheless, your reason finds plenty of adequate arguments to justify your going that way! So, when you have understood the love of God in Christ crucified, your reason is fully involved. Not to follow on then, is sin; it is sheer folly. Whereas 'the foolishness of God is wiser than men.[7]

The cloud of God's presence

Long ago, Moses and the people of God were led through the desert by following the Cloud of God's presence.[8] And we Christians, as we follow on after the Lord, are led in the same way, by the *presence* of the Spirit of God.[9] The closer we live to the 'Cloud', the more sensitive we become to the movements of the Spirit; the nearer we come to God, the more we understand His purposes, and the better He can guide us. As the prophet said: 'Your ears will hear a voice behind you, saying: 'This is the way, walk in it.'[10] Even in the darkest night, so long as we have an unerring guide, we needn't be afraid of losing the way. How good it is that we

(7) 1 Cor. 1:25
(8) Ex. 13:21–22; Num. 9:1–23
(9) Rom. 8:14
(10) Is. 30:21

don't have to depend merely on our own intelligence or instincts in order to win through to our objective! We have access to all the intelligence and energy of the One who holds the universe in being, to enable us to grasp and fulfil His marvellous purposes. Happy is the man who puts all his trust in Him!

Walking by means of the Spirit [11]

In the original text, the word 'Spirit' is used here in the dative case, without any preposition; this is the instrumental case in Greek. It should therefore be translated: 'Walk *by means of* the Spirit', that is, counting on Him, *relying on Him*'. As you depend on your feet, your muscles and your eyes when you walk, so now count on the power and intelligence of the Holy Spirit to guide you, to keep you, to open up the way, to carry you, and to lead you to the end in view. He will not disappoint you. When a little girl relies on her daddy's strength and care to get her across a mountain torrent, she is expressing her faith in him. And, in exactly the same way, the child of God is expected to rely on his heavenly Father's arm and to obey Him *by going forward*.

Walking towards an objective

Although God does not let us see all the details of the road in advance, He does not leave us groping, without a clear sense of direction. Noah had an objective.[12] So did Abraham.[13] Likewise Moses.[14] The Apostle Paul had a fantastic objective.[15] Every man of God has a purpose in life, a definite sense of direction that he has received by divine revelation. In Bible times these men were granted both a vision of God and a positive call, which came to most of them while they were still young. After that, their whole life was directed towards the fulfilment of that purpose. They often did not see how it could ever be attained, but they set out in faith and never lost sight of the goal.

(11) Gal. 5:16
(12) Heb. 11:7
(13) Heb. 11:18, 10
(14) Heb. 11:27
(15) Acts 9:15; 26:16–18

And they got there! You also need a call, an objective, a definite purpose. Aim high; seek from God Himself the real meaning of your life; and then *walk*, push forward in that direction. Step out!

You are like a traveller who can see, from very far off, the town or the mountain towards which he is making his way. The contours of the road in front of him are often hidden; he can perhaps only see the first mile or two, or possibly only a few yards ahead. But he does not lose sight of his objective; he knows where he is going. It was in this way that Abraham set out to do the will of God, without any idea how he was going to achieve it; but he had an unshakable purpose that has influenced all subsequent history.[16] He did not know how he could have either the promised son or the promised land; but he eventually brought into the world the people through whom both the Bible and the Christ have come to us. Moses likewise, facing the great dictator of his time, had no idea how God would deliver his two million brothers and sisters from their appalling slavery; yet they *were* delivered. So Paul also, when he left Antioch, did not really know how or where God was going to use him; nevertheless he brought the Gospel to Europe and, as a result, bequeathed writings to us that are worth more than all the uranium in the world.

' . . . And you will not fulfil the desires of the flesh.'[17]

This is the marvellous way of deliverance! To those who walk by the Spirit, God promises freedom from the evil desires of the old nature. See also Paul's profound thoughts in Romans 8:2–3 on this subject. If we will only accept Christ's authority, His blessed 'slavery', we are delivered from the appalling slavery that results from the authoritative power of sin. The power of His Spirit nullifies the power of the sin-urge.

The Bible does not give us a merely negative teaching. God knows that we cannot conquer sin by ourselves, that is

(16) It is a remarkable fact that our modern world is a cockpit of the conflicting ideas of Moses, Mohammed, and Marx – all descendants of Abraham – not to speak of Christ!

(17) Gal. 5:16

why He tells us to *overcome evil with good*.[18] It is not enough
to fight against our evil desires; we must do something
positive *instead* of these things. By choosing to do the will
of God and by pressing on in this direction, you are acting
positively. When you do what God wants, the Spirit of God
takes hold of your faculties and your energy and gives them
a positive direction: you are left with neither time nor
strength to do evil. Thus your old nature is progressively
stifled and subdued by the superior strength of the Spirit of
God within you, acting upon all your 'members' or faculties.

The most terrible of sins

The opposite of faith is *unbelief*. In God's sight, unbelief
is the most terrible sin of all because it is deadly, mortal.
The reason why men go to hell is simply because they reject
God's generosity or 'grace'; it is because they do not believe
that the blood of Christ is of any value. So, in the case of the
child of God also, it goes without saying that unbelief is the
most dangerous of sins. It can rob him of all his blessing
now, and also of his reward when Christ comes into His
kingdom.

'So we see that they were unable to enter *because of unbelief* . . . The message which they heard did not benefit them,
because it did not meet with faith in the hearers. For we *who
have believed* enter that rest . . . Let us therefore *strive* to
enter that rest.'[19]

This is God's formula: '*Keep walking by means of the
Spirit and you will not fulfil the evil desires of the old nature*.'[20]

Push forward, brother! *Advance*! Get a move on!

Conclusion to part II

Let us sum up the three spiritual principles:

1. 'Grieve not the Holy Spirit of God' (Eph. 4:30).
This means *instant repentance*, with confession of all known
sin, and the acceptance of God's instant forgiveness as
Father. (1 John 1:9)

(18) Rom. 12:21
(19) Heb. 3:19; 4:2, 3, 11
(20) Gal. 5:16

2. **'Quench not the Spirit'** (1 Thess. 5:19). This means *instant obedience* to Christ.

3. **'Walk by the Spirit'** (Gal. 5:16). This means *instant faith* in Christ.

The man who lives according to these divinely-given principles, these three commandments concerning the Spirit, will surely discover the meaning of the other commandment: 'Keep getting filled with the Spirit' (Eph. 5: 18).

Part III

THE FOUR DISCIPLINES

PROLOGUE

We have now examined all the commandments contained
in the Bible concerning the Holy Spirit: the first, requiring
us to be filled, and the three others indicating the conditions
of this fullness. We have seen that all these truths converge
in a single issue: faith in Christ.

Our faith, however, can be rendered null by a soiled
conscience or a stubborn will. The three principles we have
studied – *Repentance* (which involves the confession of our
sin), *Obedience* and *Faith* – are really one principle. It is
faith that saves us, not repentance or obedience; but true
faith, being the work of the Holy Spirit, is always accompanied by true repentance and true obedience. So these
three commandments come to fulfilment in a single act.
They are like three steps up into the presence of God, only
they have to be taken in a single stride, by an act of faith.
The essential thing is to believe in Christ with all your heart.

These three principles are the three main pillars that
sustain your spiritual life. They are, as we have seen, like
the three 'boards' which make up 'the table' of your life; or,
if you prefer to think of it that way, the Lord's table. We are
now going to examine the four secondary pillars, or, if you
like, the four 'legs' of the table. The table itself is more
important than the legs; but without the legs it would not be
of much use! These 'table-legs' are the four supports, or
habits, or practices, which help us to maintain a high standard of spiritual life. They are *disciplines*, which every child
of God should cultivate with the utmost seriousness. Without
them, our faith remains infantile and has no real hope of
developing. But when our faith is backed up and nourished
by such a life of practical discipline, we can really grasp the
fullness that God offers us in Christ, and thus advance ever

further. These four disciplines or supports of the spiritual life are: *Prayer, the Word of God, Fellowship*, and *Witness*. The Bible has some very profound things to say about these things; and this will, I trust, become evident in the following chapters.

Why four?

Anyone who is weak in one or other of these four forms of discipline becomes a burden to his brothers. A table or chair that has lost a leg is very unstable, like the 'wonky' Christian, who becomes discouraged or annoyed at every little problem that arises. He is a 'difficult' man; you always have to be careful not to upset him!

There are also a lot of believers who seem to try and get by like a table with only two legs to stand on! That kind of Christian needs at least two other brothers right beside him to keep him upright. Then there are some believers, alas, who are so weak that they resemble a table or chair with only one leg or none at all! Such a person needs a whole platoon of men to hold him up. He is a hindrance, a crushing load for any church.

Is such discipline really necessary?

To be successful in anything at all in life, you need discipline, and most of us accept the fact without question. Every child from babyhood upwards has to submit to it, first in his family and then at school; without discipline, he is doomed to be an ignoramus and a social misfit.

Discipline is the basis of all useful knowledge. At school, the adolescent learns at last to discipline *himself*, to control his tendencies, and develop his abilities; otherwise he has no hope of passing his examinations. At university, success really depends on the degree of discipline and knowledge already acquired by the student. Every athlete, musician, painter, skilled worker, or scientist has to subject himself to a rigorous discipline if he wants to succeed in his particular sphere of work. Every calling requires an apprenticeship. Every young couple, when they set up home, soon discover the need for a very firm discipline in their life, for without it their marriage breaks up, and their children turn out failures.

An undisciplined nation is always at the mercy of the one that is disciplined; all history confirms this.

Why then, when it comes to the things of God, are believers generally so undisciplined? All too often they think they can succeed spiritually in spite of a good deal of slackness. This is absolutely false. It is sheer folly, for such people expose themselves to the intense malice and power of the enemy of Christ. Since all sensible people accept the idea of discipline even for the things of this life (and without it nothing valid is achieved), it is obvious that we need discipline in the matters of the kingdom of God! We can hope for nothing in the spiritual realm without a committal of our entire being, involving all our abilities and all our means. Failure to recognise this is, in fact, a lack of elementary spiritual intelligence. Why indeed did Jesus call those who believed in Him 'disciples'? *A disciple is a man who is disciplined.* If you have no discipline in your spiritual life, you have no right to consider yourself a disciple. Happy is that man who accepts the discipline of Jesus.[1] He will really get somewhere.

(1) Mt. 11:29–30; Lk. 14:25–33

8

THE OPEN HEAVEN

The first discipline:
The miracle of prayer

Why prayer? Now that you have eternal life, you are in direct touch with the Source of the universe, with God Himself. The development of real intimacy with Him is undeniably the most important thing in your life. I can find seven basic reasons for this.

1. *Prayer is direct contact with God.*
It is the *only* activity of man that brings him face to face with the Creator. All other activities operate on the 'horizontal' plane, from man to man. Prayer is man's only 'vertical' activity; it is the dialogue of his soul with the One who gives him life. In fact, we could say without exaggeration that the whole purpose of God's saving us is *that we may pray*. God is the Source of our soul's light, He is our spiritual Sun. The flower cannot exist without light; it opens and turns avidly towards the life-giving rays. So, in the same way, the child of God turns towards God, praying spontaneously, inevitably drawn to the Source of his being. Prayer is the essential, supreme experience of the believer's life. Every other activity is secondary to a man's prayer life.

Prayer is living. All that will remain of our spiritual life after death is, in a way, our prayer life – in other words, *our real knowledge of God*. The more this is developed now, the richer we shall be in the kingdom of God. It is only in as far as we know God today that we can really serve Him, not only now, but also after the return of Christ. We cannot communicate to others more than we know ourselves. Both Jesus and the apostle Paul teach that our reward in the kingdom of God will correspond to the development of our spiritual life on earth.[1] Prayer is therefore absolutely basic.

(1) Lk. 19:11–26; 1 Cor. 3:11–15

2. *God commands us to pray.*

The Bible contains a very large number of injunctions to pray. Jesus said that men should always pray and not give up![2] In the garden of Gethsemane He asked His disciples, with a breaking heart: 'Could you men not keep watch for one hour with me? Watch and pray so that you will not fall into temptation.'[3] Paul said: 'Pray without ceasing.'[4] God commands us to pray night and day – this one reason should be a sufficient inducement for us without all the other powerful reasons that follow.

3. *All the men of God in sacred history were men of prayer.* We see this all through the Bible. The story of their call, their vision and their message makes very exciting reading; it is a fascinating study. To discover their secret is to possess the supreme treasure. So far as we can tell, all these men had an extraordinary experience of God, and most of them entered into it while they were still young. They had an intimacy with their Creator which we still envy, even today. Their faith, translated into prayer, many times changed the course of history. Read, for example, the lives of Moses and Paul and then compare your prayer life with the experience of these men. Why should not you also have a similar experience?

Moreover, *all the men of God throughout the history of the church were men of prayer.* You really must read the lives of Hudson Taylor, George Muller, John Bunyan, David Brainerd, C. T. Studd, John Sung, Sadhu Sundar Singh, John Wesley, to mention only a few. All were men of prayer, spending a great deal of time each day face to face with God. And they achieved almost unbelievable feats for God.

4. *Even the Son of God Himself, while He was on earth, needed to pray!*

In fact, He prayed much more than other men. I used to think He could do that simply because He was Son of God, and even that, as Son of God, He could have done without it; but it is evident from Scripture that *He really needed to pray.* This was because He was also man (and not a 'superman' or angel). Even before starting His ministry, He spent

(2) Lk. 18:1 (N.I.V.)
(3) Mt. 26:40, 41 (N.I.V.)
(4) 1 Thess. 5:17

forty days of prayer and fasting in the desert. In so far as He was human, He needed to grasp the issues clearly, get His message clear, confront the devil in person and overcome him by the Holy Spirit. After that time of solitude, Jesus came back amongst men filled with the Spirit, and with a shatteringly powerful and simple message. All through His three years of spiritual work and teaching, He was constantly escaping into the hills and lonely places to pray, before facing the crowds again. If the Son of God had so much need of prayer, how much greater is my own, seeing I am only a man and a sinner at that! And what about your own need?

5. *It is in prayer that faith becomes operative.*
Jesus made it stark clear all along that we can expect nothing of eternal value without faith. But faith remains inoperative and useless so long as we don't pray. Prayer is the inevitable *expression* of faith, the vehicle of faith. If I believe the promise of God, I simply have to grasp it forcibly, and use it. Otherwise I reduce it to meaninglessness. What is the use of saying I believe the Word of God, if I do not actually put God to the test, if I do not *require* Him to keep His promise? If I have a cheque in my hands, it is not enough to believe simply in its validity: I must cash it, or it remains valueless. So prayer consists in 'cashing' the promises of God. It stakes everything on the Word of God. 'Faith comes . . . by the Word of Christ.'[5] Faith becomes operative or active when, by the Spirit, it takes hold of the divine statements and promises. But if I do not pray, *really* pray, my faith remains inert. In other words, I fall into unbelief.

6. *When you pray, the Spirit of God goes into action.*
It is in response to your faith that He operates. When He acts, the evil spirits in the 'heavenly places' have to yield, vanquished by the authority of Christ.[6] When you pray, a whole 'chain reaction' is set in motion in the invisible world. The Spirit of God puts the Word of God into effect; He applies the value of Christ's precious blood to your prayer. He uses and vindicates your faith.

7. *God loves you: that is the ultimate reason for prayer.*
When you love someone, you want to be with that person.

(5) Rom. 10:17
(6) Eph. 1:3, 21; 2:6; 6:12–18

The presence, the voice, the face of that man or woman has become absolutely necessary to you. Love cannot endure absence; love cannot be satisfied with less than a total relationship. But who can measure the love of God, the desperate love that was manifested on the cross of Christ? If we can begin to understand how much God wants us to be with Him, in close fellowship, against His heart, we shall understand also the reason for prayer. I think of prayer as a 'dodge' that God has invented in order to drive us ever back to Him, ever nearer to His heart. Prayer is the inevitable expression of love; and it is love that gives life its significance.

Does prayer need a pattern?

There is in man an innate tendency that drives him to distort the truth of God. In the same way that he ruins the earth with unmitigated exploitation, and the pollution that accompanies it, so man twists or invalidates the realities of the faith.

In all the history of Christianity, I think nothing has been so distorted as the concept of prayer. Religion has all too often reduced prayer to a rigid formula or a mere rite, depriving the believer of that spontaneity, that *reality* in his fellowship with God and with his brothers which makes all the difference. To impose such limitations on a man does him a great wrong. Do you think that any man, opening his heart to the girl he loves, really wants to express himself in a set formula, in a sort of ready-made liturgy of prescribed words? Why then do men treat God in that way? Is it because they don't know Him? Prayer, actually, is the language of love. It is the thirsty soul's longing for the face of God.

Nevertheless, even the Word of God reveals that prayer is not really formless. As with the tree, the flower, the cloud, and the baby, each having its distinctive form, so the relationship between man and his Creator inevitably assumes a certain 'shape'. But this form has all the spontaneity of life, all the infinite variety of the fruit of the Spirit of God.

The seven phases of prayer

I find seven distinct aspects of prayer in the Bible, and we can summarise them as follows;

1. Petition or asking.

This is what I call the 'baby' or elementary phase of prayer. Like a little child, we ask of God according to our needs and our desires: we want His protection and help, we want Him to solve the problems of our work, money, friendships, health, marriage, and all the rest! Every day we 'bother' God with our little concerns. And God replies. Like a mother, He loves to see His child come to Him at all times of the day, wanting something from Him. Even a really harassed mother would rather have this than find her child avoiding her. God allows us to have all these needs and difficulties for the very purpose of encouraging us to pray, to drive us into His arms.

2. Confession of sin.

We cannot, however, get any further in prayer until we have put our accounts right with God. We need to examine our conscience, and face up to the searing light of His gaze, for 'God is light and in Him is no darkness at all.'[7] Jesus taught His disciples to begin their prayer with these significant words: 'Hallowed be Your name'. So, as we approach God, we need to come afresh to the cross of Christ, for we cannot enter God's presence with any other argument than that the precious blood of His Son answers for our sin. But God's heart is open to this argument; and, once our conscience is cleansed, He instantly assures us of His fatherly forgiveness.[8]

3. Thanksgiving.

Under the law of Moses, the Jew, after offering the 'sin offering', that is, the sacrifice for the expunging of his sin, was expected to bring a 'thank offering' to God. He needed to *thank* God for forgiveness, as for everything else. The New Testament reminds us constantly of the need to thank God. The Lord's Supper, or Breaking of Bread, is essentially an act of thanksgiving, the expression of our gratitude for the sacrifice of Christ. The first disciples at Jerusalem broke bread from house to house every evening, so conscious were they of what Christ had done for them. Undoubtedly God's

(7) 1 Jn. 1:5
(8) 1 Jn. 1:9

heart is deeply wounded when we forget to thank Him for the blessings He gives us.

When you are really discouraged, the best thing you can do is to start thanking God! There are a thousand reasons for being grateful. When I begin thanking God, I never get to the end of the list! When Paul and Silas were in prison at Philippi, exhausted with suffering, lying on their lacerated backs among the vermin, and with their feet high in the stocks, they found the best thing to do about it was to thank God! And soon they were singing His praises; You know the rest of the story![9] Even if the whole world is against us, God is for us and we have heaven before us. For every minute of suffering, we have an eternity of joy.

4. Praise.

From gratitude to praise is only a single step. The spiritual, victorious Christian is constantly praising God with all his heart. God does not want what most men call praise, the flattery that comes merely from the lips; He hates it as much as we do. To praise God is, essentially, to recognise the truth about Him. In other words, it means seeing clearly! When I have a true vision of God, I begin to realise how great He is, and how extraordinary is His grace and compassion. I see how utterly marvellous is the Christ through whom He created the cosmos and Who, on the cross, opened God's hidden heart to me. Praise is simply the reaction of the human soul in the face of a vision of sheer reality. We are dazzled by it, amazed beyond words. The truth of God is so fantastic, that, when we recognise it and express our heart-thoughts to God, we utter what the Bible calls praise. It is the flowering of a soul that sees God and is overwhelmed with love for Him.

5. Adoration.

Adoration, or worship, goes beyond praise. It is that instant when, overwhelmed with the revelation of Christ's face, our heart flings us at His feet, and we have no thought but for Him alone. God then becomes our all; we exist only for Him; our soul is transported by His beauty and His love. It is the moment when we give ourselves wholly to Him.

Oh, what a fragrance this is for God! I cannot help

(9) Acts 16:24–34

thinking of Mary of Bethany, a few days before Jesus' death, when she broke open that flask of perfume that was worth as much as a whole year's wages, and poured it out over her Master's feet.

6. Communion.

'Our fellowship [or 'communion': the original Greek word means 'sharing'] is with the Father and with His Son Jesus Christ.'[10] This means that I share everything with the Father and the Son. My soul finds the very purpose of its existence in a satisfying union with God. This is the ultimate significance of prayer.

The Lord's Supper is the perfect symbolism of this communion. In the crucifixion of His Son, God has expressed the total gift of Himself; and now, inevitably, He looks for the reciprocal gift of my own self, of all that I am. To give His whole being without reserve into God's hands is the purest joy that man can know. God's Spirit thus brings me to the point where I can have, in common with Him, all that He loves. And this 'all' can be summed up in a single word: Christ. That is heaven!

To be in fellowship with God means to be conscious of His presence night and day. Whether in conscious prayer, in meditation on His Word, in witness or in work, in weariness or joy, at the factory, at the office, in the family, in the street, everywhere, God fills my thought. My feet are still firmly planted on this earth; I even do my work better than before, and all my senses are fully awake; but the light of God's face floods through my whole being.

7. Intercession.

Here, at last, we reach the absolute summit of prayer. God wants us near His heart, but not only for our own happiness; He wants to make us conscious of those millions of human beings for whom Christ died and who are still lost in the dark. Jesus said that there is more joy in heaven over a single sinner who repents than over ninety-nine just persons who need no repentance. God's heart breaks for the salvation of this lost world. As we penetrate into this holy intimacy with Him, we begin to understand His unutterable grief over humanity; it weighs on our heart, it becomes an agoni-

(10) 1 Jn. 1:3

sing burden. We begin to enter into something of the mystery of Calvary. We suffer with God at the thought of those who know absolutely nothing of the marvellous blessing that God has granted to us. We find ourselves praying for them, interceding for them.

In the Old Testament, the 'priest' was the man called by God to stand between Him and the people. It was the priest who, with the blood of the sacrifices, had to pray in the sanctuary for those outside and obtain their pardon. In the New Testament, all believers are called to be priests; we all have that marvellous right of access into the presence of God, and we are *all* called to pray for those who are outside. The supreme privilege open to a human being is that of entering into the presence of God for the sake of a fellow being, a lost soul. And his supreme happiness consists in leading that soul to the knowledge of God. As the Apostle Peter says, we are 'a holy priesthood';[11] and, as John says, Christ has made us . . . 'priests to His God and Father'.[12]

There is one thing you must never forget: *as a child of God, you have instant, direct access into the intimate presence of God by the blood of Christ.*[13]

The true meaning of prayer

As our knowledge of God deepens, we understand how great is His desire to become fully involved in our life. Jesus said: 'Seek *first* the kingdom of God and His righteousness, and all these things [the material things] shall be yours as well.'[14] When we realise that the revelation of God's face means more to us than anything else in the universe, our prayer comes to maturity. God says: 'Seek *My face*.'[15] Christ said to Martha: '*One thing* is needful.'[16] And Paul said: '*One thing* I do . . . I count everything as loss because of the surpassing worth of knowing Christ Jesus my Lord.'[17]

(11) 1 Pet. 2:5
(12) Rev. 1:6
(13) Heb. 10:19–22
(14) Mt. 6:33
(15) Ps. 27:8
(16) Lk. 10:42
(17) Phil. 3:13,8

This kind of prayer takes us beyond the 'infancy stage' of wanting 'things' or mere 'experiences', towards a quest for God Himself. It becomes a flame of adoration, an unceasing communion, a continual dialogue with the Eternal One. It is being 'together'. It is the realisation of His presence, the meeting of our spirit with His Spirit. God longs to remove any veil that may come between us, any sense of distance, any doubt or lack of trust. He wants us to be truly united with Him, of one heart and soul. Our prayer is simply the means God uses to throw us into His arms, so that He may draw us to His heart. If we did not need to keep asking Him for all sorts of things, most of us would neglect prayer and remain tragically far from the intimacy He seeks from us. But through our desperate need to importune God con-tinually, we find that He attracts us to Himself, in order thus to bring us into deeper and deeper fellowship with Himself.

In the Greek New Testament there are several words corresponding to the English word 'prayer'. Two of these, in the original, mean a *desire* and a *need*.[18] Prayer is essen-tially a desire. It is first of all a desire to have something or other; and, in the end, it becomes the desire to have God Himself, to be intimate with Him, to be all His. But when this desire becomes a *need*, our prayer passes beyond the elementary to the mature stage. It takes us 'through the veil'. It becomes an imperative, urgent cry. We can no longer take 'No' for an answer. Our need of God has become desperate, absolute. This word 'need' is generally translated in English by the word 'supplication'. God demands that we persevere in prayer *and in supplication*.[19] Persevering means reaching to the limit, going right through to the ultimate. Reaching God's heart. Seeing it through with God. This is when God begins to use us on behalf of others.

The conditions for answered prayer

The New Testament gives us a clear definition of the conditions upon which God answers our prayers:

The General Condition.

Jesus promises that, if we ask anything *in His name*, God

(18) In Greek: *proseuchē* and *deēsis*, as in Phil. 4:6
(19) Eph. 6:18

listens to us and gives it to us. For example, in John 14:13–14 and 16:23–27. But what does it mean to 'ask in the name of Jesus'? All too often, people suppose it is enough to utter the formula 'in the name of Jesus' or 'in the name of Christ' at the end of a prayer, for God to answer them automatically. But praying 'in the name of Jesus' really goes far, far beyond that.

To act in the name of anyone, you have first to identify yourself with that person. A girl for example, when she marries – at least in most northern countries – takes the name of her husband from that time forward; she is identified with him by bearing the same name. She can sign documents for him. She lives in the same house. Her children also bear his name.

To ask 'in the name of Jesus' means *to identify yourself completely* with Jesus, with His thoughts, His desires, His objectives, His will. It means you can use His name, or His 'signature', for the simple reason that God Himself reckons you are identified with Him. We now seek His interest alone – knowing, all the same, that He really only wants our true, eternal happiness. When our life is 'one' with that of Jesus, God tells us to ask to the uttermost, because the very thing He wants most of all is to fulfil the wishes of His Son! The Spirit of God thus turns our thinking towards the desires of Jesus, and Himself works with the object of bringing them to pass.

The Three Specific Conditions

At the beginning of the 'ideal' prayer that Jesus taught us,[20] we discover the three basic conditions which we all need to observe if we want God to take our prayer seriously:

1. '*Hallowed be thy Name*'. As we have already seen, this means we must approach God with a clear *conscience*, with sin confessed.

2. '*Thy kingdom come*'. This is an act of *faith*. God expects us to believe He will in fact accomplish what He promises.

3. '*Thy will be done* on earth as it is in heaven'. This is the aligning of our *will* with that of God. He expects us to obey Him with all our heart.

(20) Mt. 6:10–13

We find the same three conditions laid down in Hebrews 10:19-22, where God calls us into His presence: 1. 'With a sincere (or true) heart', that is to say with a 'whole' or *obedient* heart; 2. 'in full assurance of *faith*'; and 3. 'with our hearts sprinkled clean from an evil *conscience*'.

What is striking and yet completely logical, is that these three conditions for answered prayer are the same three conditions that God requires of us for the fullness of His Spirit: 1. *Repentance*, accompanied by confession of sin; that is, a good conscience. 2. *Obedience*; that is, the acceptance of the will of God. And 3. *Faith* in Christ – a faith that really goes forward!

We find these same three principles all through the Bible, even, for example, in the symbolism of the Levitical sacrifices instituted by Moses.[21] There is nothing surprising in this, for, as I have clearly stated, these three principles are all summed up in one word: true *faith*, purified from an evil conscience and an evil will. When we are fully at one with God, nothing prevents our taking hold of His promises. And prayer is the logical and inevitable expression of such faith.

Do you realise that heaven is open before you? At the cross of Christ God's very heart was opened to you. What holds you back, what prevents your reaching out to the uttermost with God?

An additional condition for collective prayer

When it comes to united or common prayer, the Word of God adds a further condition. Jesus promises His disciples the answer to their prayers as a community on condition that they *agree*, that they are really united in heart and objective. This promise should be read in the context of the whole of Matthew 18, where Jesus insists on the need for a true unity among children of God. An absolute oneness of ideas and doctrine is not really possible on this earth, but Jesus is speaking here of a unity of heart and purpose. 'If two of you agree on earth about anything at all they ask, it will

---

(21) In the 'burnt offering', all was given to God; in the 'sin offering', the conscience was cleansed of guilt; in the 'thank offering', faith took hold of God's forgiveness.

be done for them by My Father in heaven.'[22] It is in this spiritual unity that the presence of Christ is manifested and prayer is answered. In a nucleus of such Christians, there is an ultra-atomic power. It is God touching the earth.

How much time should we allocate to prayer?

The New Testament leaves us free. Each individual must work out the details of his prayer life with God. However, I remember that, as a young Christian, I myself made very little progress in my spiritual life until I agreed to give God a tithe (that is, a tenth) of my time. That meant almost two and a half hours each day. At first it seemed impossible to find all that time in one day; yet I desperately wanted to know God in an altogether new way. After months of hesitation and conflict, I was able to make a covenant with God about it. For forty years now God has honoured this agreement.

I began by asking God to meet me specifically three times a day, in the early morning, at noon, and in the evening. I found in the Bible that Daniel did this, and that he felt it better to let himself be thrown to the lions rather than give it up for even a single month.[23] I fully understood that, just as my body needed three solid meals a day, my soul also needed three adequate spiritual meals a day! I found a day of twelve hours was too long without a break to meet God. I decided to give God *enough time to speak to me*.

Naturally enough, I found it difficult to fit in all this time in three long sessions; so, all through the day, I 'grabbed' a minute here and two or ten minutes there, in order to make up my 'tithe'. But it was unspeakably precious to be able to forget the world completely three times during the day and to concentrate all my thoughts only on Christ. I certainly found it hard going at first; but after a few months, these rendezvous with God became more and more radiant. Finally He brought me into such an intense fellowship with Himself, my intimacy with Him became so deep, that I found I was praying all day without ceasing, not only in my leisure time, but even in the midst of hard intellectual work. I often went

(22) Mt. 18:19
(23) Dan. 6:10, 16

out of doors to pray; I found that walking easily became 'walking with God', and I gained physically as well as spiritually by the experience!

Prayer doesn't necessarily have to express itself all the time in articulate speech; it can also be a spiritual 'state' in which we are in continuous communion with God, as with someone you love. Two lovers don't have to keep talking all the time to convince each other of their love; the very fact of being together is everything. God longs to bring us into that very relationship with Himself, when we love to be in His presence and we long for His face.

The New Testament fixes no rule about the amount of time we should give to God. We are completely free in this matter. But if we are wise and if we really love God, we shall naturally give Him as much as possible. Our time is, in fact, the *most precious* element at our disposal, and, if we are wise, we shall economise it for God. It is worth far more than money, for you can sometimes get back lost money, whereas you can never recover a wasted hour or minute.

The Jew, under the old covenant, gave God a tenth of his money and of all his income. The Christian is under no obligation in the use of his money; but he would be crazy to give God less than the Jew gave. Everything we give to God becomes an eternal treasure in His kingdom; the wise Christian lays up all the wealth he can in heaven in order to have greater treasure at Christ's coming. We have only a limited number of days and minutes on this earth. This time is infinitely precious. It goes without saying that the time given to God is the most valuable investment possible to man. Most people nowadays spend at least the tithe of their time looking at their television! Shall a disciple of Christ give less than that to his God?

You are a child of God; you are free; God does not treat you as a slave. But be intelligent, as intelligent as possible.

9

THE INFINITE DISCOVERY

The second discipline:
the treasury of the Word of God

Jesus, faced with all the power of Satan in the wilderness, put him to rout with these words: 'Man does not live on bread alone, but on every word that comes from the mouth of God.'[1]

You only have one life to live on this earth. As I have said, your time is infinitely precious; you do well to make the most of it. In a few years' time, unless Christ comes first, you will no longer have eyes with which to read, nor a brain with which to understand, nor hands with which to write. The Book of Ecclesiastes says: 'Remember *now* your Creator in the days of your youth, *before* the evil days come.'[2] If now, while you are still young, you come into a deep knowledge of God through His Word, then your whole subsequent life will be set in a valid direction from the start.

The thinking-process of the world around us is in flagrant contrast to God's own thought. Men's accepted ideas and their false values invade us from every angle, stunting our spiritual development. It isn't easy to get rid of them. Everywhere, truth seems to be mixed up with error. We are conditioned and contaminated, a lot of the time unconsciously, by the things we see and read and hear. Every single day we need to be cleansed afresh and set right. Our mere conscience is not enough to guide us; it is like the compass needle that does in fact point to the north, but never to true north; there is always a magnetic variation, which needs to be corrected repeatedly by constant reference to the mariner's chart. So our conscience needs to be constantly corrected by the voice of God, by reference to His Word.

(1) Mt. 4:4
(2) Eccles. 12:1

God fully realises our problem: that is why He brought into being (and at what a cost!) the Book in which He defines His own thought-process. It is a most accurate statement; in fact, it is the only source of absolute truth we possess.

How has the bible come to us?

From beginning to end the Bible claims to be the Word of God. He took at least two thousand years to create it, using some forty authors of most varied character, from a whole gamut of different backgrounds, men who had, for the most part, no possibility of knowing one another. Among them are found kings, philosophers, statesmen, poets, peasants, fishermen, nomads and priests. It is really a library of sixty-six books, a comprehensive literature of immense significance and spiritual wealth.

Yet this book possesses an organic unity comparable to that of a human body with its almost unbelievable complexity, but entirely inspired and controlled by a single divine intelligence, as the body is co-ordinated and directed from the brain. For many reasons, the Bible is the most remarkable book the world has ever seen, the more so as it contains no scientific error or absurdity in spite of its great antiquity.

The first page of Genesis is by itself evidence enough of its divine inspiration, for the correlation between the phenomena listed in this chapter and the fundamental conclusions of science at the present day is staggeringly accurate. Not only are the facts stated correctly, which is something almost incredible when you compare the Genesis account with *all* the other ancient cosmogonies, or accounts of the origin of the world; but even the chronological order in which they are enumerated is just as accurate. This is utterly fantastic, for the author of this document, which is several thousand years old, had only one chance in over 25,000,000,000,000,000,000,000,000 of getting this order right; yet he has, in fact, arranged all the details correctly! I enjoy asking an atheist to explain that!

Most impressive of all is the Bible's inherent quality of authenticity, its ring of truth that convinces us that it is the Word of God. In every country and in each generation, it meets man on the level of his deepest need. As we read this Book, we hear the voice of God speaking into our moral consciousness; it penetrates to our inmost heart, and contains the power to transform it into the image of God.

The difference between reading and studying the word of God

I distinguish between *reading* and *studying*. It is simply not possible to study the Bible seriously without first knowing its contents. It is just like trying to write a book on Einstein before knowing his work. The very first thing we need to do is to become familiar with the entire text of Scripture; and the only possible way of doing that is *to read it*. There is no short cut to this end.

It is impossible to get a real grasp of its contents if you read it too slowly, or in irregular 'chunks', or if you let it 'slide' for a time. Our very first need is to read it *right through* several times in order to get a comprehensive view of the whole. Fortunately, it is a book that a man can read daily all through his life without ever getting tired of it. The overall view you obtain by such straight reading then makes it possible for you to go deeply into the details of its contents; and this opens the way for studies of infinite richness, both exhilarating and of lasting value.

Let me explain!

This I can best do through my own personal experience.

God met me when I was nearly eighteen years old. The first year of my new life was marvellous, but then I lost my spiritual power and joy, and my life became progressively more disappointing until I was twenty-three, when I was almost in despair. No one had taught me that I needed to read the Bible systematically. But, fortunately, I did read, during that time, the biographies of several great men of God – among others, those of Hudson Taylor, Charles Studd and Robert Chapman. The life of all these men made a profound impression on me.

I also perceived, in certain people I knew and who were exceptionally used of God, a quality of life which was quite out of the ordinary. All this led me to search for the secret of that kind of life. What struck me most deeply about all these people was their intimacy with God: they had a knowledge of Christ which was beyond my experience.

In the biographies I had read, I saw that all these men of God, without exception, had two points in common: they all had a well-developed prayer-life, for they all began each day alone with God; and, secondly, they all read the whole Bible through, each year, taking the two Testaments concurrently. Eventually I became convinced that the secret of their success lay in these two things.

That year, when God took the tenth of my time, I disciplined myself to read the whole Bible through consecutively, taking the two Testaments together, beginning with Genesis and Matthew, and reading right through to the end in one year. I shall never regret that decision!

At first, I found all this discipline pretty tough going. But after a few months, it ceased to be hard; it became an unspeakable joy. God began to reveal Himself to my soul in a way no words can describe. I was living in the radiance of a heavenly dawn that grew daily more and more overpowering and infinitely beautiful; to me, it was the very springtime of God, transforming all my own thought-processes. The light of His face flooded through my whole being: I was beginning to live in heaven; I was dazzled by the revelation of His love.

The first time I read the Bible right through, I confess that I found many things quite beyond my grasp; certain passages astonished me, even shocked me. However, I committed these matters to God each time, and persevered with my reading. At the second and third readings, as I began to understand the whole scope of the Book, a good number of these difficulties disappeared; and, year by year, the ideas that once were unintelligible to me became more and more clear and marvellous.

After I had read the Bible through several times, I began to discover a positive pattern in God's thought, a sequence in His revelation. I could now follow the development of His purpose from the beginning until His final issue at the end of time. I traced His intentions through the history of the nations, and particularly that of Israel and of the church.

I was discovering a new universe, the kingdom of God itself. I could now see things from God's point of view; the Bible became an extraordinary book. I seemed to be climbing an exceedingly high mountain, each month reaching a fresh summit from which I had a vast panoramic view of the whole cosmos, including the invisible world. Everything fell into perspective. I could see where all the various roads led; the world's tumult seemed relatively insignificant; the nations, with their ideologies and their quarrels, appeared like ants in comparison with the greatness of God. This vision, which grew continuously, brought me an inward serenity that made me conscious of God's immediate presence in the very midst of my most difficult daily occupations, even in time of war and the most terrible grief.

What was even better, this panoramic view of the whole Word of God helped me to see its different components and details in their true setting. Doctrines were made clear from Scripture itself; the many aspects of sin were shown up with pitiless clarity; my faith was constantly being developed and enriched; the thousand marvels of Christ, and His unutterable beauty, blazed before my eyes. God co-ordinated, in my thinking, a great many truths that previously had seemed confusing or even contradictory. Life, and the universe itself, assumed greater and deeper significance.

I wouldn't want you to miss such a blessing for anything in the world. I know I am being very insistent about these things, but it is because I know their value. I have never met anyone who regretted seeking God and reading the Bible in this way. On the contrary, I know a lot of people who now do this very thing, and they all tell me it has transformed life for them.

Reasons for reading the Bible

Read it for sheer pleasure. Decide, first of all, that you are going to *enjoy* reading the Bible. It is a romance, an almost incredible spiritual adventure, the story of the search for man by his Creator. I would even say that it is the love-story in which He opens His heart to you personally. The most Holy Spirit who inspired the Bible has also created the spring flowers, the mountain snows, the Milky Way, the face of a little child, and the miracle of love. To read the Bible is to set out each day on a fresh adventure with God; you find yourself exploring the fantastic landscape of His kingdom, and you will be infinitely rewarded.

Read the Bible to know God. The Bible exists for the express purpose of revealing God. We therefore read the Bible, not to acquire a mere 'head' knowledge of its contents, although that in itself is of inestimable value; but in order to get to know its Author. The Bible is the road that leads us to the true God, the God of Jesus Christ; for it is only through the Bible that we know Jesus. If you read the Bible, crying to God to reveal Himself, it will become the mirror in which you see His face.

If you read it merely in an intellectual way, as a bare academic study, you cannot hope to find anything but sterility for your soul, for the mind by itself cannot reach God. The mind and the spirit are meant to function together.

But the opposite attitude is just as unfortunate, the attitude that refuses to bring to the study of the Word of God all the intellect and other resources which God has put at our disposal. It is God who created man's mind, when He made him in His image. What God wants is to make a *whole* and balanced man of you.

Read the Bible to maintain your prayer life. Prayer and the Word of God go together. They are like the two wires of a telephone conversation which make it possible for us both to listen to God and to speak to Him. The spiritual life is meant to be a dialogue with God. The more we listen to the voice of God and grasp the things He wants to reveal to us, the more our prayer becomes inspired and permeated with faith. His Spirit thus turns our hearts towards the things of God, and our praying consequently becomes more and more effective. The man who neglects the Bible finds that his prayer-life becomes feeble and tends to disintegrate. We need to listen to His voice most carefully. God longs to see our hearts open to Him.

Read the Bible to nourish your soul. Your body needs a regular and balanced diet; it stands to reason your soul needs the same thing, and to an even greater degree. There are many Christians who lead a mediocre spiritual existence because they neglect the Word of God; they are 'undernourished'. If you are a poor eater, you inevitably become debilitated. Just as the body needs three good meals a day, morning, noon and night, so, as we have already said, your soul needs the Bread of life regularly. Do not deprive yourself of your daily sustenance.

Read the Bible to strengthen your faith. 'Faith comes . . . by the Word of Christ.'[3] The faith you now possess was created

(3) Rom. 10:17

in you through the Scriptures; the Bible is the very source of
your faith. If you want God to develop it, you will have to
draw deeply from this spiritual well. Our faith actually comes
into effect when we rely on the Word of God; the Bible is the
very rock-bed on which our faith rests, for, as I have said, all
our knowledge of Christ derives from it. The more we know
God's Word, the better we shall know His will, and the more
shall we be able to rely on Him.

The Best way to read the Bible

Read the Bible with prayer. 'The natural [or animal] man
does not receive [or grasp] the things of the Spirit of God, for
they are foolishness to him and he cannot know them,
because they are discerned *spiritually*.'⁴ To approach the
Word of God with your mere intellect is therefore folly. We
depend on the Author of the book, the Holy Spirit, to teach
us its meaning. We need to ask God's help each time for the
understanding of its message; but God will not fail to give it
to any who approach Him in a spirit of honesty, humility and
faith, relying on His Spirit.

Read the Bible every single day. God said to Joshua: 'This
book of the law shall not depart out of your mouth, but you
shall meditate on it *day and night*, that you may be careful to
do according to all that is written in it; for then you will make
your way prosperous, and then you will have good success.'⁵
And Joshua did, in fact, have good success!

Moses commanded the kings of Israel to make a copy of
the Law and to read it *all the days* of their life.⁶ The kings who
did that, like David, were truly successful. God also said:
'Blessed is the man who meditates on the Law of the Lord
day and night; he is like a tree planted by streams of water; in
all that he does, he prospers',⁷ whereas other men are carried
away like chaff by the storm wind.⁸

The great men of God never let a day pass without reading
the Scriptures deeply.

Read the whole Word of God. All heresies and false doctrines

(4) 1 Cor. 2:14
(5) Josh. 1:8
(6) Deut. 17:19
(7) Ps. 1:1–3
(8) Ps. 1:4

are based on isolated passages, taken out of their context without regard for the rest of the Bible. People who use the Bible like that can twist its meaning in any direction they want. That is the way Satan quoted Scripture when he tempted the Lord Jesus in the desert. It is dangerous to restrict yourself only to parts of the Bible. Did not Jesus say that 'man shall live on *every word* that comes from the mouth of God'?[9] Your aim should be to know it from beginning to end.

The Bible contains God's complete revelation. So to content yourself with mere fragments of it is to deprive yourself most terribly; you commit a crime against your own soul. Think of the many persecuted believers in other countries who would give anything to possess a Bible! Yet we, who actually have it in our hands, seem all too often to find it a bore. The tremendous privilege of having access to this treasure makes us all the more responsible in God's eyes.

By reading the whole Bible, we put ourselves within effective reach of the whole action of God's Spirit. He is thus able to teach us 'all things', as Jesus promised;[10] every day He can correct us, enlighten us, and lead us into further truth; He has the means to protect us from the devil, the world and the flesh; and, by degrees, He opens up to us more and more of the secrets of God's heart.

Begin with the New Testament. I strongly advise a beginner to leave the reading of the Old Testament till later, and to concentrate all his attention *at first* on the New Testament. There are two reasons for this:

(a) The New Testament material is absolutely basic. It is of immediate and vital concern to the disciple of Christ, for it contains the words of Jesus Himself and of the apostles who knew Him. If we may say that any part of the Bible is more important than the rest, then, without any doubt at all it is the account of the teachings and the life, death, and resurrection of the Son of God that constitutes that element. Jesus Himself tells us to begin with His own teachings, that is, the four Gospels.[11]

(b) The Old Testament, while it is equally inspired of God,

(9) Mt. 4:4
(10) Jn. 16:13
(11) Mt. 7: 24–27; 28:20

and equally relevant to us, is concerned in the first instance with Israel. It is difficult to grasp its full significance for us without some previous knowledge of the New Testament, after which it becomes readily understandable, and eventually exciting and infinitely rewarding. I therefore recommend the consecutive reading of the whole of the New Testament two or three times before beginning the Old.

Then read the two Testaments concurrently. I advise you to begin simultaneously with Genesis and Matthew, and carry on from there every day. There are huge advantages in this method, but the most important one is that you get a *balanced* spiritual diet in this way. The New Testament contains the spiritual 'vitamins', or rather 'proteins', so necessary for our health and for promoting rapid growth. I often think of the New Testament as our 'spiritual beef steak', and the Old Testament rather as the 'vegetables'! They are both necessary and they are complementary; but the proteins are of primary importance in building up the tissues and nerves. You should never let a day pass without studying the New Testament. By reading the two Testaments together, you avoid spiritual 'indigestion', and that barrenness and weariness that overtakes some Bible-readers. In this way you can maintain your appetite, and there is less risk of your riding a spiritual 'hobby-horse', or having a 'bee in your bonnet', to the exclusion of other truths which are equally important.

Read consecutively. No one can master a language or a science by studying haphazardly, with no real method. If I begin today studying a book at page 179, and then return tomorrow to page 3, then, the day after, skip off to page 65, and then on to page 200, how ever can I hope to grasp my subject? My knowledge will always be fragmentary and disjointed; it will probably even be dangerous. What a lot of Christians tackle the Book of God in that way! It is really asking for trouble.

In the Bible there is a positive sequence of ideas, not only chronological, but also logical, or rather spiritual. It begins with the creation of man and culminates in the great day of judgement and the new creation. To grasp the whole is to be able to interpret the details correctly. Such an over-all conception saves us from spiritual instability, and from inaccuracy and exaggeration – tragic failings that divide and impoverish the work of God all over the world.

You need an objective

If you do not have a definite objective, you will end up being discouraged; your reading and your prayer will become difficult, and probably sterile; you will 'lose the thread'; the deeper meaning of the Bible will escape you. Worse still, the things of this world will crush out your soul's desire for God; and, too late, you will discover how difficult it is to recover your first love once you have lost it. It is indeed possible to find it again – but at what a cost! On the other hand, if you really commit your way to God, and persevere, He will keep you truly orientated, and He will maintain your spiritual vision.

Your first objective: the whole New Testament

So I recommend, first of all, *the reading of the whole New Testament right through.* If you read an average of three chapters each day, you will accomplish this in three months. One chapter in the morning, one at midday, and one in the evening (or as God directs you) – that will keep you in good shape all day, and will fill your heart with tremendous things to think about. You will be astonished at the spiritual progress you make.

After that, I advise you to *repeat* this experiment! Thus, in six months you will have read through the whole New Testament twice over! You are then quite well equipped to deal with a host of problems and emergencies. And you have some really potent answers to the questions people fire at you.

The ideal objective: through the Bible in a year

Your second objective should be to read through *the whole Bible in one year,* reading the two Testaments concurrently and consecutively.

If you do not read as fast as that, you will find it very difficult – and I think even impossible – to obtain that overall strategic view of the Scriptures which is so necessary for the understanding of their true meaning.

When I set myself to read the Bible systematically, I reckoned that I should have to read *three or four chapters each day,* almost three times as much of the Old Testament as of the New. I found, surprisingly enough, that almost anyone can in fact read a chapter of average length in five minutes! That means that, with *twenty minutes' daily reading*, you can get completely through the Bible in a year. Show me the man who isn't capable of that!

But, of course, I was not satisfied with only that. As I reckoned on giving God a tenth of my time, I had at my disposal, not only twenty or thirty minutes for basic reading, but *another two hours for pondering, exploring, and studying the text, and for prayer*. Much of this time I spent out of doors, as I have already said, for the Lord Jesus, when on earth, often went into the open country to pray. Such a discipline opens the door to infinite possibilities.

You think it is too difficult?

I very well know that the road I am setting before you is tough going. It is, in fact, humanly impossible. The world system is so contrived by the devil as to exclude Jesus Christ from life; everything is against you. I know it from my own experience. All through my life, I have had to seize time forcibly, grasping it between two jobs of work, or in a bus or a train or a café, or before or after a meal, sometimes while eating, or when walking down the street, or, when necessary, by getting up earlier or going to bed later. But, if you are in love, you manage well enough to fit in time to meet the girl or the boy you love! And so, when you have really fallen in love with God, you somehow or other find time to spend with Him. Where is the man or woman who can't rob the day of half an hour to study the eternal truths?

Ask God to fix the objective for you. If you really cannot follow these suggestions, then ask God to show you what He really wants of you, the objective at which He really wants you to aim. It is God Himself who must decide on the use of your time, and He does it according to His loving-kindness. God knows what you need and He also knows your limitations and your capabilities. He thoroughly understands your circumstances. He is not trying to devour or exploit you; He is your Father, most tender and compassionate, and He wants your true happiness. You are free. The New Testament does not lay down any rule about this matter. But be in earnest about it. Your life is slipping away; it is trickling through your fingers even as you read these words. And you have only one life to live.

If you simply can't make it by yourself, the Scripture Union offers simple Bible readings with excellent explanatory notes. This is a very good beginning, especially for children and 'starters'. But if you really want to go far with God, you need more than that, and *nothing* can replace the *consecutive* reading of the Scriptures. The Scripture Union offers you a plan for that too. There is nothing, of course, to prevent your following the Scripture Union or a similar course of reading while at the same time following the method indicated in this book. Though you may find that complicates things rather a lot.

Reckon it up!

Some folks say to me: 'What you are postulating is an impossible target; you really expect too much! Why, the whole Bible in one year! That is perhaps all right for some intellectuals; or for people with time on their hands; but, as for me, I reckon that to read the Bible through in five years is an adequate objective!'

To that I reply: 'Yes, to read the Bible through in five years is not bad. But just figure this out accurately. Let us say you are twenty years old and that you have just met God. Now, if you read the Bible through in five years, that means that, at the age of twenty-five, you will have read it once, but only once. That is well enough as it goes; but think a minute! At the age of twenty-five, you are a man or woman at the peak of your strength and with all your faculties developed. You should be in the forefront of the new generation, a man or woman who can see very clearly, who knows the answers, who can now readily discern the true from the false, and who can above all inspire the adolescents who are growing up around you. Yet you have only read the Bible once; you are hardly even a beginner in the things of God. You are still in God's nursery!

At the age of thirty, you may have two children, perhaps three; the eldest will have begun asking you a lot of questions and will already be causing you some anxiety. Your home will be invaded by problems they bring home from school and from the street. In your church there will be young people needing someone who understands their difficulties, and can face their spirit of revolt and their questions with divine wisdom. But you have still only read the Bible twice; you yourself are still at primary-school level so far as the things of God are concerned; you are hardly out of the kindergarten. Yet you are thirty years old, at the very summit of your vitality. Mature, no doubt, in everything but the ways of God.

At the age of forty, you are expected to carry the whole burden of the world on your back, including your adolescent family and the church with all its problems. This is the age when a man should be able to achieve his masterpiece. But you have read the Bible through only four times; you are still a mere spiritual 'adolescent', possibly even somewhat retarded, since your progress has been so slow. You are still poorly equipped, you do not have much of value to contribute to the agonising problems of the new generation which is now coming to full age. Instead of being the chief of a thousand in the army of Christ, you are still only bringing up the rear.

Then, at the age of sixty, you will have read the Bible only eight times; you will still be hardly adult. You will have read it so slowly, that you will have forgotten a great deal of its contents each time before beginning again. Why, a man of sixty should be a father of the church, a wise man, knowing all the answers, capable of imparting deep teaching, and able to confront the agonising and critical problems of the men of forty years of age, as well as those of younger people. Today, there is a terrible dearth of such men, for the simple reason that they were not taught when they were young to give sufficient time to God, in order to know His Word.

All that is the negative side. *Now let us look at the positive side.* If you read the Bible in approximately one year, it means that, at the age of thirty, you will have read it through ten times! You will already have a deep knowledge of the things of God. Already you will be saturated with the whole range of His thought. You will have a surprising strength, you will already be a man of God. Then, at the age of forty, you will have read the Bible through twenty times; you will have become a veritable prophet or teacher; you will have a positive message for the rising generation; you will be a source of inspiration for your children; you will be a pillar of the church. And, when you reach the age of sixty, you will have read the Bible through forty times! You will now have an invaluable and stunning message for young and old. You will know how to give the church of Christ a true direction and save it from error. You will have an inexhaustible wealth of truth to communicate. Instead of fading into an insignificant retirement in old age, tragically forgotten, you will be sought out from all sides because of the heavenly light you can shed on basic and current questions. Oh, my brother, my sister, how I covet you for God, that He may make of you a man or a woman of God! In all eternity you will not cease to bless God for this!

Bible-study develops out of Bible-reading

I have said that you can't really *study* the Bible until you have read it and know what it is all about. But once you have gained a thorough knowledge of the actual text, you are then in a position to *examine* it in depth. Such a study becomes infinitely rewarding, amazingly significant, as the Spirit of God links up the various truths and facts of Scripture in your thinking. Without this knowledge of the entire text, you deprive the Spirit of the full use of His sword, which is the Word of God.[12] You limit His revelation of Christ.

There are many ways of studying the Bible. Each believer in the end must discover for himself the method that suits him best; but he needs to use *all* the means God puts at his disposal; then he can decide on the best procedure.

There are, however, certain basic principles which, I am convinced, are indispensible for everyone. Once you have mastered these, you can go on building that foundation according to your own individual needs.

The purpose of your *reading* is to get to *know* the whole content of Scripture, the actual text; whereas your *study* has as its aim the *understanding* of the text – and that is the work of a lifetime! At eighty, you are still learning with all the gusto of a baby!

It is the Spirit of God who enlightens our mind. It is therefore essential to approach the Word in a spirit of prayer and with real humility, for God resists the proud but gives grace to the humble.[13] We must have a mind that is always open

(12) Eph. 6:17
(13) 1 Pet. 5:5

to the truth of God *and is willing at all times to be corrected by it.* 'He who ignores instruction despises himself, but he who heeds admonition gains understanding.'[14]

Some practical suggestions for study

As you read through your New Testament or Bible for the second or third time, you will be surprised at the number of passages that you have forgotten. Although God has spoken to you at different times in one place and another, all too often you lose these precious thoughts; they escape your memory. So it is a good idea to have a pencil with you and underline or mark those passages where God speaks to you. Then, not only can you find them more easily afterwards, but the very fact of marking them fastens them in your memory. When you read them next time, they hit your eye immediately. In my own experience I discovered that, after reading the Bible for a year or two in this way, a great number of marvellous passages had become woven into my thinking-process; they were now an integral part of my soul. *I realised with astonishment that God was beginning to think through my brain!* All through the day, my soul was flooded with the light of His face. This revelation remained constant with me, even in the midst of my daily work. The Spirit of God was building a vision in my own spirit, a knowledge of God in depth, a conception of Christ that began to transform my life.

You will very soon need *a good Bible,* well printed and well bound, preferably with wide margins, so that you can make notes to your heart's content. It will probably be a good thing to have a pocket-size edition as well, that you can carry around with you everywhere you go. To help you to get a grasp of the geographical and historical background of the Bible, you will also need a good *Atlas* of the Bible and a good *Bible Dictionary,* of which several exist in English. This will enable you to find, at a moment's notice, the information you need about the name of a person, or the history of a country or a locality; it will help you to pinpoint obscure details in the Bible and explain terms or allusions which you find too difficult. These and other similar books may be expensive, but they are infinitely worth the cost, since you possess them

(14) Prov. 15:32. See also 10:17; 12:1,15; 13:1, 10, 13, 18, 24; 17:10; 19:20; 23:12

for years, and maybe for your whole lifetime. They are a veritable mine of information about the Bible. It is useful to have a real grasp of the history and geography of the Bible. The only thing is, you mustn't let these *helps* take the place of the Holy Spirit in your study. The all-important thing is to get to know *God Himself*, face to face; and only His Spirit can give you that revelation.

The background knowledge you gain as you go along will not only make the study more interesting and understandable, but will often shed valuable new light on the text itself. For example, when you realise the social and international situation in which Isaiah found himself, and against which he lived and worked, you are absolutely staggered at his vision and message. This is true of the work of all the prophets, and equally true of that of the apostles in the New Testament. We find their message extraordinarily relevant, brilliantly focused on our own contemporary situation!

After having read the whole Bible through two or three times, you will begin to feel the need of *classifying* your discoveries. The Bible deals with many subjects. Personally, I use a colour system for marking my Bible, and I always have a pack of coloured pencils with me for this purpose. I mark or underline each major theme with one particular colour throughout the Bible. That enables me to co-ordinate, in my mind, the teaching of the whole Bible on that subject. Just to give you some idea of the possibilities, I will mention here the way I distinguish some of the more important themes. You, of course, do not have to follow this literally! You should rather work out a system suitable for your own needs.

Yellow: the return of Christ, the restoration of Israel, the rapture of the church, the kingdom of Christ, heaven.

Orange: chastisement, judgement, hell.

Red: the blood of Christ, salvation, the new birth.

Purple or grey: sin.

Black: Satan and all his work, including particularly demonic sins such as idolatry and occultism.

Green: the inner life of communion with God. I also include here the idea of grace, forgiveness, and love.

Dark blue: the outward life, obedience, witness, perseverance, persecution.

Sky blue: God, Christ, the Holy Spirit (I use three distinct shades of this colour!)

Violet: the Word of God, truth, inspiration of Scripture, faith.

Brown: practical questions, discipline, church matters.

Of course, these subjects often overlap, and in any case there are not enough colours in the rainbow for the hundreds of subjects dealt with in the Bible! I have used every possible shade of each colour, but even so there are nothing like enough colours! So I have also invented a system of symbols and initials placed in the margin, by which I can convey a more precise definition. By this means I can group together the different passages dealing with, say, a specific sin, or a particular aspect of the return of Christ. For example, wherever the Bible mentions the sin of the tongue, I put a 'T' in the margin while underlining the passage itself in purple, the colour I use for that kind of sin. The sin of anger is indicated by the letter 'A' in the margin; and so on. But I strongly advise you to simplify all you can! You will get tied up in knots if you complicate things at the start. I myself began with only one colour; then I found the need of a second colour; subsequently I developed the system as the need arose – not before!

There are some huge advantages resulting from such a system of Bible marking. For example:

1. You can rapidly acquire a balanced and comprehensive knowledge of all that God says about the different subjects that interest you and seem important to you.

2. You avoid the danger of becoming eccentric or lopsided.

3. At almost the first glance, you can spot any passage you are looking for in the Bible.

4. You have an ever-growing fund of material, not only to improve your own study, but also to communicate to others in preaching and witness and counsel.

A well-annotated Bible becomes a treasure beyond price, and is an indispensable tool not only in your witness to the world around you, but also in your daily living. But after a time, you may find that such a Bible has one great disadvantage. As you go through it again and again, you tend to fall back into the same old thoughts instead of discovering a whole new series of truths each year. If your Bible is 'saturated' with notes, I advise you to get a new one and start again from the very beginning. This will allow God to bring you completely fresh revelations. I myself use my annotated

Bibles for preaching to other people, but I usually start a new Bible for my own use each year or so! I learnt this from the example of C. T. Studd and other such men whose lives I had read.

Then you will need, from the outset, *two note-books*. I find loose-leaf ones best, as you can remove useless pages, and rearrange your material as your work improves.

In the *first* of these note-books I advise you to write (if possible in a single sentence or two) *each important new revelation* you receive from God. From time to time, when you are on your knees, or reading your Bible, or in a meeting, or even walking down the street, a sudden illumination comes to you from God; but you will find you generally forget it if it isn't immediately written down. It is a pity to lose such a valuable truth. When you take the trouble to write it down, not only is it retained, but it becomes clearly defined, and thus a valuable sharp-edged weapon in your spiritual armoury. *An idea that is not expressed in words remains vague* and often impossible to grasp. But, when crystallised into precise language, it becomes part of your soul.

A *second* notebook is needed for what I call *classified references*. For example, reading your Bible today, you were perhaps struck by a verse on the prayer of faith. At the same time, the Holy Spirit brought to your mind also two other verses on the same subject. If you don't want to lose all that, you can then open the notebook and head a page with the title *Prayer of Faith*; and, underneath it, you jot down the references for these three verses. They need not be quoted completely, just enough to make the meaning clear. The next day you come across a striking passage about the return of Christ; so you start a second page with the title *Return of Christ*; there you note the reference, with perhaps that of five other verses which the Holy Spirit brings to your memory. Eventually, you find you are compiling a little personal concordance, but with this supreme advantage, that all this information has come to you, not through the brains and experience of someone else, but straight from God. All these passages will become part of your thought and experience. You don't need to complicate things. Keep everything as simple and basic as possible, or you will find yourself out of your depth and your study will become too involved for you to keep it up.

There are *two advantages* in having such a system of classification:

1. Your notes and markings in the Bible itself, as well as the classifying of the references, will enable you to develop a very clear, balanced, and comprehensive *grasp of doctrine* or Bible truth.

2. In a few years' time, you will have a very powerful *spiritual equipment* in your possession. If, one day, you are asked to preach, or witness, or lead a Bible-study, you will have a wealth of material at your disposal. As you fall on your knees and cry to God for inspiration, the Spirit of God can answer with a good range of truths to communicate through you. Supposing he tells you to preach on the prayer of faith: you look up the passages that have impressed you and moulded your life. From these you choose first a key passage and back it up with a number of others. Then, when you come to preach, instead of merely reasoning or even 'waffling' around a text or two, you read your principal passage and then drive home the truth with text upon text, each one coming out with the full impact of the experience that God has burnt into your own soul. It is your very heart speaking; or rather, it is God speaking through your whole being. The world desperately needs to hear that voice.

How can we be sure of interpreting Scripture correctly?

It is an unspeakable joy to discover truth; all Bible-study should lead us to this end. But God says that the heart of man is deceitful above all things and desperately wicked.[15] It is difficult for any man to be absolutely straight and honest; every one of us has an innate tendency to twist the meaning of Scripture in his own favour and to reach wrong conclusions. That is why you find so many different interpretations, often quite contradictory, almost everywhere you go. It is not because God's revelation is inadequate; it is because most people don't take the trouble to discover what the Bible really says, and they mix up their own or other men's ideas with God's actual statements. That is where all the trouble comes from. That is what divides Christians.

To guard against this danger, we need to discipline our-

(15) Jer. 17:9

selves very carefully. We need a firm attachment to God's Word itself. We need a heart utterly open to the truth and willing to accept whatever God in fact says. We need to aim at one hundred per cent honesty. For this to be possible, we must submit all our prejudices and preconceived ideas to the ceaseless scrutiny of that light, and ask God at all times to correct anything in our thought or doctrine or behaviour that is not in conformity with His Word. If we study the Scriptures with such an attitude, we can confidently expect God's Spirit to lead us into all truth, as Christ promised.[16] 'God is light and in Him is no darkness at all.'[17] Let us therefore walk in the light and then we shall not stumble. God hates dishonesty. He calls it lying and He calls Satan the father of lying.

To make sure I didn't 'cheat' in my own Bible-study, I decided to check all my conclusions by the three following basic principles of interpretation. If you want likewise to maintain an attitude of absolute honesty in your approach to Scripture, so that God can really guide you into all truth, I believe you need to do the same.

The three principles of interpretation

1. *Nothing but the Word of God.* We have no right to interpret God's Word by any authority other than itself. The Bible is in itself the final authority because it is the Word of God. We must therefore put on one side our personal prejudices, and all the traditions and reasonings of men, including the interpretations of any individual leader or spiritual movement whatsoever, and search out honestly what God Himself says. If you approach the Bible wearing 'coloured spectacles', or ecclesiastical or doctrinal 'blinkers', you are in fact putting a human authority on a level with that of God. But God does not admit of a rival. Don't forget that the Lord Jesus was rejected in the name of the Word of God, simply because He came into conflict with the 'Tradition of the Elders' – that is, with the system of interpretation of Scripture then in vogue among the scribes. They held their interpretation to be just as important as the Scriptures themselves; whereas, in the eyes of Christ the Word of God was the *only*

(16) Jn. 16:13
(17) 1 Jn. 1:5

authority, and that is why they crucified Him.

I don't mean by this that all other reading should be excluded or that we should not listen to preaching! Let us accept from God all the means of learning which He offers us; but let us refrain from *interpreting* His Word by any authority other than His own. Thus we can receive with gratitude everything of value that men like Augustine, Calvin, Bunyan, George Müller and hundreds of others can tell us; but let us be careful not to subject the Word of God to their authority. Every human being is fallible; every truth which comes to us through man is to some extent distorted, just as the sunlight loses certain rays when it passes through a pane of glass. The light glancing through your window is a delightful experience; but the flood of the clear, pure sunshine out in the open air is a hundred times better.

So, when it comes to defining Biblical truth, it is essential that we limit ourselves to the inspired Scripture itself. God forbids us to add anything to His Word.[18]

2. *All the Word of God.* The Bible contains all the spiritual truth that is necessary for man. Error is almost always a half-truth. We are constantly exposed to error if our conclusions are based on isolated Bible passages. That is where your system of Bible-marking and notes and classification will be so exceedingly useful, for in this way God will be able continually to *correct* your ideas, and to teach you the whole range of His truth. When you are really acquainted with the *whole* text of Scripture, the Spirit of God can then begin to build a *synthesis* of the different aspects of a subject. The truth of God is the Bible *as a whole*. To define any Bible doctrine, it is imperative that you take into consideration 'every word that proceeds from the mouth of God', as Jesus said. *Subtracting* from His Word is just as disastrous as adding to it.

3. *The Word of God interpreted by itself.* The Bible explains itself. God is perfectly capable of making Himself understood. For every topic in the Bible, there is at least one passage which is absolutely clear, and which, to the honest heart, allows of only one interpretation. Such a passage must therefore be taken as the key by which to interpret other relevant passages where, for some reason or another, the

(18) Deut. 4:2; Rev. 22:18–19

meaning is less clear. The Bible does not contradict itself. If you come across an apparent contradiction, you must search the whole Bible through prayerfully for its explanation. When we sincerely ask our Father to teach us, His Spirit will help us to locate the passages we need and fit them together.[19]

What we should never do is take a verse or a sentence out of its context, and build our theology on that! All the false teachings that claim to be Bible-based indulge in this kind of sophistry. It is fiddling with the Word of God. Anyone who manipulates the truth like that is walking on the very edge of hell.

God is light, and He looks for an honest and good heart in which to sow the seed of His Word.[20] We need to be humble enough to admit our ignorance, and patient enough to wait on God until He makes things clear. As for me, I had to read and search the Bible through from end to end some ten, fifteen, or even twenty times, before arriving at a definite conclusion on many important subjects. During all those intervening years, God nevertheless gave me all the spiritual food I needed day by day, strengthened my prayer-life, opened His heart to me, and prepared me for my life-work.

It is very good and useful to have the opinion and experience of other Christians, and especially of real men and women of God; but, in the end, it is God alone who decides on the meaning of His Word. He Who has given us a mouth and a brain knows, even better than we do, how to reason and express Himself!

I am amazed at the unity of interpretation to which, even without our knowing one another, God brings those of us who take the trouble to read and study the whole of Scripture and who learn to interpret it honestly. This is yet another sign of the authenticity of the Bible! 'Blessed are *the pure in heart*, for they shall see God.'[21]

The need for discipline

The word 'disciple' means 'pupil' or 'apprentice', a man or woman 'under discipline'. We are in Christ's school; we have

(19) Jn. 16:13–15
(20) Lk. 8:15
(21) Mt. 5:8

everything to learn. This demands time, and great earnestness. A 'disciple' is, as I have said, a 'disciplined man' – what else?

When God created our planet, He hid all kinds of treasures in the rocks: gold, petroleum, uranium, and the rest. But it is up to man to discover these things and to mine them. In the same way, the Bible contains a mass of spiritual wealth, but it has to be explored and drawn out. God does not make the corn grow of its own accord in the field; it has to be cultivated. Fuel doesn't just drop out of the sky into your engine! God supplies the birds with an abundance of food, but they have to start searching for it early in the day. The earth yields its riches to the man who really seeks them. So does God yield the incalculable riches of His Word to the man who searches them out. 'Blessed are they that seek Him with their whole heart.' [22]

A girl learning music has to go through a long period of very tedious study at the beginning. Then, one day, she finds she can actually pour out her soul through her instrument; it is the opening of a new dimension in her life. The same experience comes to anyone who studies a language; he reaches a point where he pierces through into a new world; he has a whole new culture and landscape open to him; he has access to a vast wealth of literature which was previously unknown to him. What an enrichment for his life! How much more so then for the man who perseveres in his searching of the Scriptures!

The lazy Christian will always be dissatisfied; he remains a weakling, like an under-nourished child. The out-and-out Christian will, on the other hand, marvel more and more at the increasing revelation of God. His search brings him a reward far beyond any comparison with the effort he has made. The Word of God becomes an unutterable joy, a ceaseless source of inspiration and enlightenment.

But isn't this legalism?

No, it certainly isn't legalism. Christ's Good News has freed us from the yoke of slavery – may God keep us from taking it on us again! It is rather a question of being plain

(22) Ps. 119:2

intelligent, of using to the best advantage the precious and all-too-limited time which is entrusted to us. Christ's discipline is neither legalism nor bondage; it is the spontaneous expression of love. As the young man disciplines and masters himself in order to love and help his young wife, so the disciple of Jesus desires above all else to know Him intimately and to serve Him more effectively. Remember that your great enemy, the devil, is unbelievably intelligent and that *he* is directing all his powers against you. So make full use of the resources God has put at your disposal. Be intelligent where the things of God are concerned. Be wise, be very intelligent.

What about those 'difficult' days?

Do not be discouraged if sometimes you do not seem to get much out of your reading. In ordinary life there are days of sunshine and days of rain, there are mountains, deserts and green valleys; so also, in the spiritual realm, there are all kinds of influences, visible and invisible, acting upon you. There are times when the demonic opposition is stronger than usual; there are times also when physical tiredness and the state of your health affect your inner being. The day will come, however, when these apparently 'difficult' or 'dry' readings will take on a new meaning for you. The important thing is to keep up at all costs a constant daily rhythm of reading.

Meanwhile, God will give you day by day enough truth to meet the need of your soul, even if at times it is only a verse or a promise to serve as food for that day. In the days of Moses, God provided for the needs of His people in the desert by means of the daily manna; He will provide likewise for your own needs. But remember that the manna had to be gathered *early*, for it melted once the sun became hot. That is why *we must seek God early*, before the world crashes in to desecrate the peace of those marvellous first moments of the day.

What about the 'boring' passages?

I think God has deliberately placed near the beginning of the Bible those passages which at first sight seem of no great interest; it seems to me this is done on purpose *to test us out*

(I am referring particularly to Exodus, Leviticus and Numbers). Those who are not desperate to know God, when they come up against this difficulty, turn away – to their immense spiritual loss; whereas those who persevere out of sheer thirst for God find that the Bible, taken as a whole, is an absolutely fascinating book; they are continually finding fresh spiritual resources in it. It is unfathomable. Eventually, you discover *unsuspected treasures* even in the apparently boring passages. Just as the physical universe appears infinite to our mathematical calculations and radar telescopes, so the Bible discloses an unlimited horizon, an infinite revelation of the kingdom of God, in which we discover the ultimate realities. I say this after a lifetime of experience in studying the Book of God.

An agonising choice

A few years ago, among a group of friends in Paris, I was insisting on the need and the advantages of such a discipline where prayer and Bible-study were concerned. One of my friends, who was the director of an important firm, said to me: 'You are right, Ralph, I know. But *how* are we going to get this time for God?' And he described his average day's occupations, which, true enough, didn't leave him the ghost of a chance of achieving this ideal.

My answer was something like this: 'I know, it's impossible! But we are faced here with an issue of eternal significance, an absolute priority. In the last analysis, we can't hope to achieve this miracle; only God can do it for us. But this very fact reduces us to the alternatives of sheer faith – or unbelief. We have to do with the God of the impossible. Can He, or can He not, bring to pass His will in us? If He can't, then everything we believe is rubbish.

'I know, this world has no room at all for Christ. When He enters, something else has to give way; something inevitably has to disappear to make room for Him. In order to have the best, we often have to jettison the good. Didn't Jesus Himself say it is better to get rid even of your right hand or eye rather than lose out on the essential thing? We are faced with a choice from which there is no escape. There is no question of legalism here: it is simply a matter of love. The love of God.

'The fellow who is content to spend a mere five minutes

every other day with the girl he intends to marry hasn't even begun to know what love is – any more than the believer who is content to offer God the scraps of his time.'

The devil's master key

But the problem goes really much deeper than that. If, in fact, we have to push even legitimate and necessary things out of our time-schedule to make room for Christ, what are we to say about our 'doubtful' occupations?

For example, we are informed by statistics that every baby born in the United States is now doomed to spend twelve years of its life in front of the thing the specialists call the 'idiot-box' – by which I mean the television screen. *Twelve years*! That, so far from being a tenth, is more like the fifth of a man's lifetime! In Europe, the figure may be a little less; but, even so, the average person spends something like ten or twelve hours a week – that is, one day in seven held by the screen.

A certain Christian, watching a television set being delivered to his home, noticed this slogan splashed across the crate: 'It brings the world right into your home.' In a sudden flash he saw the truth. What was, for other men, an attractive piece of propaganda, had become a deadly warning to him. He refused the delivery, and the television set went back where it had come from!

Have you grasped the fact that the devil has now found a master key that opens all doors, *your* door? He now possesses an instrument of incalculable power by means of which he can introduce his own thought-system, what Jesus calls 'the world', right into your private life. Night and day, your home and the minds of your children can be permeated with all the thinking-process of the world, taught all its philosophy and its very impurities. There are lots of 'stalwart' Christians who would never dream of walking into a cinema, yet they don't care a hoot when the cinema walks right into their sitting-room!

Our fathers did not have this problem. When they shut their front door, everything could speak to them of God; Christ was the undisputed Master of their homes. 'Don't love the world', says God,[23] 'nor the things that are in the

(23) 1 Jn. 2:15

world.' Today you, as a Christian, have to face up to this question: can you have a television screen in your home without getting soiled by the world? You can be utterly sure that, if you grieve the Holy Spirit, the presence of Christ will forsake your home. Christ will refuse to live under a roof where He is expected to breathe the same breath as Satan and listen to his unholy laugh.

Let us reason this out

'Oh, come on,' I hear somebody say, 'a Christian isn't expected to be a fanatic! You must admit that there is some pretty good stuff on the telly.'

'A fanatic?' No, the disciple of Jesus is not called to be a fanatic; God expects him to be intelligently aware and well-informed, full of common sense, with a mind wide open to the problems and opportunities of his generation, and able to come to grips with them.

Television is not, of course, an evil thing in itself. Everything depends on the use you make of it. If we could put it into the hands of Jesus Christ, it could rapidly transform this poor planet for the better. If I could use it to make Christ known to the world, I would do so; yet how few are the countries where this is even possible!

But it is not Jesus, it is His enemy who at present directs the affairs of this world and controls its resources.[24] He is the very first to realise the vast strategic potential of this weapon. For this reason I do not on any account want to be saturated with his point of view, least of all in the evening when I am disarmed by fatigue, and my family likewise.

Oh, I know! I don't deny that some of the programmes are really interesting and even very informative. But there are other programmes that are the very opposite – and how difficult it is to choose the right ones, and even more so to use the necessary foresight! *Even the 'good' films nearly all contain a negative and often destructive philosophy*, which people absorb by degrees *without even realising it*. Do you think you will escape?

The whole problem consists in mastering or controlling

(24) 1 Jn. 5:19

this 'beast'. If you don't succeed, then you can be certain that it will control *you*. The real danger lies in the *habit*, for, over a period of time, your whole outlook is profoundly altered *by the cumulative effect* of what you see and hear. We finally lose the ability to see things as God sees them. And we don't realise where we are going.[25]

Did not Jesus say that the lamp of the body is the eye?[26] It is a well-recognised psychological fact that the impressions received through the eye are the ones that penetrate most deeply and remain in the subconscious. Television gets at us both through the word and by sight, and for this reason its effect is exceptionally powerful.

The Apostle Paul in front of the screen!

Paul didn't have the problem of television to deal with in his day, but he did have a problem, in that tortured church at Corinth, with which he had to deal on the same basis. Paul devotes three whole chapters to it! You need to read the entire passage, 1 Corinthians 8–10. Only, when you come to the expression 'food [A.V. "meat"] offered to idols', read the word 'television' instead! In the place of 'eating food' [or 'meat'], read the phrase: 'watching a programme'. And so on all through! If you are at all like me, you will be astonished to find it all so contemporary, and you will be extraordinarily enlightened by the Apostle's reasoning.

It would be worth analysing Paul's five-fold argument in detail, but that would need a whole chapter to itself. This, among other cogent points, is the gist of what Paul is saying: 'You Corinthians know what immense sacrifices I made and how much I suffered in order to bring Christ to you and bring you to Christ. You know how I give up all sorts of perfectly legitimate privileges and comforts (including a wife and a home and a salary) in order to win as many souls for Christ as possible, and to avoid putting any obstacle in the way of those who are weak. It is in this way that I managed to found your Church at Corinth.

'And now you have the effrontery to ask me if you can flirt a bit with the world from which God delivered you by

(25) 2 Pet. 2: 20–22. See also 1 Cor. 12:2; Eph. 2:11–13; 4:14, 17–24
(26) Mt. 6:22–23

the blood of Christ, because you are not under the law but under grace? Don't you know anything about the value of that sacred blood?'

Paul sums up his argument thus: 'All things are lawful, but not everything is helpful, not everything is constructive.'[27] 'But I have not used any of these rights.'[28] 'We endure anything rather than put an obstacle in the way of the Gospel of Christ.'[29] *I refuse to let myself be enslaved by anything.*'[30] And he concludes: 'Do everything to the glory of God.'[31]

Brother, sister, if you can honestly look at a television programme for the glory of God, then go ahead! But, if you can't, then you must stick a gigantic question mark against it. Remember the word: 'The man who has doubts is condemned if he does it [literally 'eats'], because his doing it ['eating'] is not from faith: and everything that does not come from faith is sin.'[32]

The image of the beast

Some time ago, in America, the technicians of the firm of Coca-Cola tried out a hair-raising experiment. They introduced, in any ordinary story-film that came on the screen, the phrase 'Drink Coca-Cola', inserted after about every twentieth still. It flicked by so fast that no one had even the remotest idea he had seen it; *yet it was registered in the subconscious mind of the viewer*, with the result that the sales of Coca-Cola soared sky-high and stocks were sold right out. When the truth leaked out, the public became so scared that a special law was passed in the United States forbidding this kind of psychological manipulation.[33]

Nearly every country in the world is now a dictatorship; and the control of television naturally becomes the prerog-

(27) 1 Cor. 10:23
(28) 1 Cor. 9:15
(29) 1 Cor. 9:12
(30) 1 Cor. 6:12
(31) 1 Cor. 10:31
(32) Rom. 14:23
(33) (Ref.) See ch. 7 of 'The Church at the End of the 20th Century' by Francis Schaeffer for an interesting and frightening account of various methods of psychological manipulation at present possible or in actual use.

ative of absolute power. Even in most of the remaining free democracies, television is under a monopoly that is more or less government-controlled. Modern technique – and this applies to other media besides TV – has discovered psychological and even chemical ways of manipulating the public which are, to all intents and purposes, irresistible; and we can expect them to be applied more and more intensively each year. Unless the law specifically forbids it, those in control can now indoctrinate people in depth *without their knowing anything about it*. Satan is not blind to all this!

The Book of Revelation describes a world dictator of the End Time, who will cause *everybody* to worship him by means of *an image that speaks*![34] There is not the shadow of a doubt that he will control the television-system on a universal scale. People by then will be so conditioned by years of 'viewing' that, when the compulsory satanic programme comes across, with his hypnotic face on the screen, they will believe what they are told.[35] Can you imagine anything more logical? Or more appalling?

God leaves you free, but He warns you. You have only one life to live, and it is already slipping away. Your time is worth more than anything else. How are you going to use it? It would be utter folly to spend a fifth or even a seventh of it stuck in front of that 'box'. Isn't it infinitely better to spend a mere tenth of it contemplating the face of God?

(34) Rev. 13:15
(35) It is well known that Hitler controlled the masses principally by means of the radio and the secret police.

10

YOU ARE NOT ALONE

The third discipline:
The miracle of fellowship

You are now part of an immense, spiritual, living organism which includes all the children of God in the whole world. It is the great family of God. You are a unique and precious individual in His eyes, but at the same time you are integrated by His Spirit into what the New Testament calls the 'body' of Christ.[1] Your spiritual life is developing at one and the same time upwards in a vertical direction towards God, and also horizontally out towards His other children, your brothers and sisters in Christ. They are necessary to you, as you are necessary to them. Together we all make up a single entity in Christ. This is 'the church!'

Should we still think in terms of the Church?

If by 'church' you mean the marvellous original concept as Jesus Christ understood it and as the Apostles brought it into being in their time, the reply is a thousand times 'Yes'! But if you mean what today generally goes by the name of 'church' – well, there we really are confronted with an agonising problem.

Down the centuries men have always tended to distort the simple, clear thoughts of Jesus. The term 'church' no longer means for most of us what it meant for Him and for His Apostles. There isn't any word in the English language now that is capable of conveying His meaning; we need a completely new expression. In this chapter, I am nevertheless using the word 'church', for lack of an alternative. But I shall

(1) 1 Cor. 12:12–27

try to give the word its original meaning. Let us go back, then, to its source, to the New Testament.

What Jesus meant by 'the church'

It is Jesus who 'invented' the church. What did he say about it ? If we study Matthew 9 :35–10:42 and Luke 10 :1–20, we see how He forged and then sent out the first missionary teams. When he sent His men two by two, these men were already steeped in the teachings of the Sermon on the Mount in Matthew 5–7. This early experience in team-work was a preparation for the collective life and work of the early church as described in the Acts of the Apostles and developed in the Epistles.

Then in Matthew 13, through the seven parables of the kingdom, He put His Apostles on guard against the development of those erroneous trends in the church which unhappily all came to fulfilment in the course of history. He insisted on the need to pay any price in order to obtain the pure truth.

In chapter 16 He makes it clear that He Himself is the foundation of His church,[2] the Rock that Moses and the prophets identified with God Himself.[3]

Later, in Matthew 18,[4] when His disciples had quarrelled over the question of spiritual leadership, Jesus pronounced the 'seven laws of the kingdom', the basic principles of collective team or church life and effort, which would assure the spiritual unity of its members. In this chapter, Jesus teaches the absolute necessity of humility, especially in leaders (v. 4), and of mutual esteem and openheartedness (v. 5). He says it is better to lose your life than to stumble a younger or weaker brother (v. 6). He insists adamantly on care and respect for the weak (v. 10); on our seeking to save the lost rather than being occupied merely with ourselves (vv. 11–14); on reconciliation between brothers (vv. 15–17; and on mutual forgiveness to the utmost degree (vv. 21–35). A group or team or church that is living according to these principles becomes (as we have already said in chapter 8) an

(2) Mt. 16:17–18
(3) Deut. 32:4, 15, 18, 30, 31, etc.
(4) See also Mk. 9:30–51

extraordinarily powerful instrument in the hands of God. It is a foretaste of heaven.

The ultra-atomic nucleus!

Now let us look at the three really potent promises that the Lord Jesus includes in this passage. I take it that these hold good only for a group that is living according to the teaching which He has given us in the rest of the chapter.

First, He guarantees *the authority of His own name*, His very signature on all the group's concerted action.[5]

Secondly, He guarantees *the answer to their collective praying* because they are *united* in the doing of God's will.[6]

The third promise will take us a little time to examine in depth.[7] Jesus here guarantees *His very presence* in the midst of the group that is living according to these principles, however small the group is. 'Give me just two or three people to start with', He says. 'Where two or three are *integrated into my person*, I am there in the midst of them.'[8] I have translated that direct from the original to convey what I believe is its true meaning.

This verse is quoted almost tritely in all kinds of gatherings to justify the assumption that the presence of Christ is automatically ensured just because, let us say, several Christians happen to be singing the same hymn in the same room. The original Greek does not allow of such an interpretation. The fact of just being together, even to sing a hymn or talk of spiritual things, is a long, long way from what Jesus has in mind in this statement. The Greek preposition *eis* followed by the accusative case, in the expression 'in My name', contains the basic idea of *movement towards an objective*. For those who know Latin, the prepositions *in* or *ad* followed by the accusative translate correctly enough the Greek expression, which is not easily rendered into English. 'Into' conveys the sense better than 'in'. Christ talks about believing 'into' Him rather than believing 'in' Him.[9]

(5) Mt. 18:18
(6) Mt. 18:19
(7) Mt. 18:20
(8) Mt. 18:20
(9) Jn. 6:29, 35, 40, 47

The Greek verb *synagogein* also means more than the English 'to be gathered or assembled'. You could translate it: 'to group' (as an action), 'to draw or push together, towards a focal point'. In the whole expression, there is a sense of movement towards a centre of gravity. The situation with which we are dealing here is not a static one. It is dynamic. It is active. There is motion and objectivity.

What is this objective, this centre of gravity? It is the Name of Jesus. But what does that mean? How can one gravitate 'towards' or 'into' a *name*?

We can better grasp the significance of this expression if we remember that, in ancient times, neither Greek nor Hebrew had a word bearing the full meaning of our English word 'person'. In the Old Testament, as in the New, if men wanted to speak about a 'person', they had to say a 'man' or a 'soul' or a 'name'. You could also say a 'face'! This last expression, in both Hebrew and Greek, came to mean 'presence', and, in the days of Christ, was just beginning to be used in Greek in the sense of 'person', or rather 'individual'; but it did not convey the depth of meaning contained in our word 'person'. Thus, in Genesis 46:26, the word 'person' is the normal English translation of the Hebrew 'soul'; in Acts 1:15 the word 'person' is the normal translation of the Greek 'name', where the text reads literally; 'The number of the *names* was ... 120' (as in AV).

In the Bible, the 'name' is virtually the expression of the personality. In ancient Hebrew, the names of individuals had real significance. For example, Noah means 'Encouragement', given prophetically by his father; David means 'Beloved'; Jesus means 'Saviour'. Thus, for Moses and the prophets, the name of God was equivalent to the person of God; that is why reverence for His name was so important; it was even included in the Ten Commandments: 'You shall not take the name of the Lord your God in vain.'[10] This is why the Apostles attached supreme importance to the name of Jesus, adding His titles, 'Christ' or 'Messiah', and 'Lord' (this being the equivalent of the Old Testament name of God).

To my mind, there is no question that Jesus, whose thinking had as its background the Old Testament, identified His name with His person. When He authorised His Apostles

(10) Ex. 20:7

to pray in His name, He was actually offering them a total identification with His person. Even today, when you are allowed to use the name or signature of someone in a position of authority in order to further your interests, you are, so to speak, identifying yourself with that person for the time being. Thus it is to the extent that we identify ourselves with Jesus, with His person, His interests, His desires, His will, that our prayer is answered and our work becomes effective. To ask in the name of Jesus means to accept a total identi- fication with Him.

That is why, for lack of any better vocabulary, I translate Matthew 18:20 thus: 'Where two or three *are integrated into My person*, there am I in the midst of them.' I am absolutely convinced that this is the meaning Jesus Himself intended to convey in this sentence. It means being 'welded together' in Him, organically united, as the branches are all a part of the tree itself.

Such a nucleus of believers is a real outpost of Christ's kingdom in this hostile world, a veritable dwelling-place of God on earth. It is the kingdom of God in miniature. And it is the presence of Christ in this group (whether of three or thirty or three hundred) that constitutes the essential 'church', as He intended it. Without that presence, the group is a mere caricature of a church, a gathering of people with more or less the same interests, flaunting the title of 'church' but without unity of heart or cogent witness. The world, more- over, is not convinced by it. It doesn't matter how impressive an organisation or building you have, or even if your doctrine is very correct; unless everything is centred on the real and effective presence of Christ, it is not an authentic church – any more than a pretty wrapping is a gift, if the precious engage- ment ring it was meant to contain has disappeared.

I have taken some time to analyse this verse, because this thought is the very heart of Christ's teaching about the church, and the basis of the whole Biblical concept of spiritual fellowship.

The great commandment of Jesus

The night before His death, in the upper room, the Lord Jesus instituted the New Covenant, symbolised by the Last Supper, speaking of His broken body and shed blood. Then, immediately afterwards, we see Him on His knees on the floor, washing His disciples' feet! When He had done that, He announced (I think it was with tears in His eyes) His 'New Commandment', the 'New Law' that accompanies the New Covenant: 'Love one another,' He said, 'as I have loved you. It is *by this* that all men will know that you are my disciples.'[11]

That same night, Jesus called this new Law '*My* Commandment' – that is, His supreme commandment.[12] Without the shadow of a doubt, the most important thing in the whole New Testament, the most important thing of all in His eyes, is that we, His disciples, should love one another as He has loved us. And He loved us enough to be crucified for us.

If we understand this, God can do *anything* in our midst. In this way we constitute a true church, as Jesus understood it. The details can be decided upon later, since we already have the essential. But a 'church' that does not have this spiritual presence of Christ, which is self-evident to all comers, uniting all the brothers in a genuine fellowship or sharing, is only a parody of the truth. Where there is no unity of heart the glory of God, the 'shekinah,' is missing. The portrait of Christ offered to the world is a wretched caricature that convinces no-one and even invites contempt.

Christ's marvellous idea: The explosive cell

The Son of God is the Architect, not only of the church, but also of the cosmos.[13] It is He who 'invented' and created the electron, the atom, the molecule, and also the biological cell. And it is a fact that everything that exists is constructed on the basis of *unity in complexity*.

The church, as Jesus conceived it, resembles an atom, or, still better, a living cell, the complexity and unity of which are almost unbelievable. Still more extraordinary is the cell's capacity for reproduction: one fertilised human cell multiplies itself, in a mere nine months of pregnancy, no less than 120,000,000,000 times; and that, not haphazardly, but in such a way as to create the marvel of a baby with all its personality and the organic complexity of a human being.

(11) Jn. 13:34–35
(12) Jn. 15:12
(13) Col. 1:16–18

One has only to think of the formation of the eye during this relatively brief period to realise what a stupendous miracle this phenomenon is. Why on earth do the philosophers not believe? Paul well said that the world, with all its wisdom, simply does not know God, and that the foolishness of God is wiser than men.[14]

Now Jesus, in creating the church, never envisaged an administrative organisation, but on the contrary a living organism, a real 'body', a group of spiritual 'cells' in full reproduction. He wanted to fill the world with little living spiritual cells, each possessing the explosive power of His presence.

Nothing is said, in the New Testament pattern, of a hierarchy; on the contrary, Jesus washed the feet of His disciples and taught them that the greatest in His kingdom was to be humble like a child and everybody's slave.[15] He Himself gave us the example.

How we men distort that simplicity of Christ! The beauty of His soul is obscured by our mass of reasonings, our traditions, our interpretations, our hesitancy. The apostles were able to put His teaching into practice because they took it seriously, at its face value. They never quibbled at it.

How the apostles applied Christ's teaching on the church

It was the apostles who actually founded the church. The study of the writings they have left us is therefore of the utmost importance. It is Paul most of all who writes about it, thanks to his incomparable experience. In the Acts, we have the clear, contemporary account of it all, collected and put together by one of the men whom Paul converted and taught, Luke the doctor. There we see the simplicity and the integrity with which the first Christians lived out the teachings of Jesus, so much of which Luke himself has communicated to us in his other book, the Gospel. Then Paul, in his extraordinarily rich and intelligent letters, the 'Epistles', analyses and defines the application of this teaching in practice. What a fantastic study!

In a mere fifteen years or so, Paul had managed to fill all the

(14) 1 Cor. 1:21, 25
(15) Mt. 18:4; Mk. 9:35

countries between Palestine and the Adriatic Sea with
young, multiplying churches.[16] However did he accomplish
such a stupendous feat? I have no doubt at all that the
secret of Paul's success lay in his concept of the apostolic or
missionary *team* as Christ had taught it, and as he lived it
out in witness and suffering, first with Barnabas, then with
Silas, and eventually with Timothy and a constant succession of young men from the churches he had founded.[17]
Paul's team was at all times a dynamic mobile *cell*, filled with
the Holy Spirit, burning with love, ready for anything, and
possessing at all times the priceless treasure of the presence
of Jesus. Through its action, young churches, local *cells*,
were born in a minimum of time wherever the team went;
and these churches inherited from Paul's team the same
vision, the same life, the same dynamic power to reproduce
themselves on every hand by an endless 'chain reaction'. If
all the disciples of Christ today would take this Biblical
concept seriously and put it into practice, God would
certainly transform, not only the whole church itself, but
the very world situation.

For Paul, the church was not a static concept. It was not
in the least identified in his mind with a building of brick or
stone, for Roman law in any case nearly always forbade the
possession of any place of public worship for Christians
over a period of at least 200 years after Christ. The church
was 'in your house',[18] or in the catacombs – it mattered not
where, so long as the Spirit of Jesus was present. All the
Apostles shared this ideal of simplicity; Peter himself, in his
Epistle, considered the church to be a living organism, a
'spiritual house' whose stones were the believers themselves.[19]

The body of Christ

In 1 Corinthians 12 (especially vv. 12–27), Paul compares
the assembly of believers, the Christian 'group' or sum
total of members, to a *body*. He calls it the body of Christ.

(16) See his colossal statement in Rom. 15:19, 23
(17) The New Testament notes the names of some nineteen team-mates
of Paul, and there must have been many more. See, for example, Acts
20:4.
(18) Ro. 16:3–5: 1 Cor. 16:19; Col. 4:15; Phil. 2
(19) 1 Pet. 2:5

The human body is characterised by a perfect unity in spite of its breath-taking complexity. The whole body is directed by a single mind or intelligence and controlled by a single nerve-system. Yet it is made up of an astonishing variety of members and organs, nearly all of them with very different functions.

It is the same with the church. Christ is the Chief, the Head.[20] He is the 'brain', the centre of His body's nervous system. We, the people of God, are the members, the 'limbs', the many 'organs' of Christ. As in the human body, so in the true church we find an extraordinary complexity, yet conceived in perfect unity. The body of Christ, in its many members, has in fact a marvellous variety of functions. Listen to these God-inspired statements of Paul:

'*The body is a unit, though it is made up of many parts* ['members' or 'organs'].'[21]

'*You are [together] the body of Christ and individually members of it.*'[22]

'*We have all been integrated* [the Greek word 'baptised' in this context means 'immersed' or 'plunged' or 'inserted'] '*by one Spirit into one body*' (v. 13, correctly translated according to the original). Here there is the idea of a graft[23] of the branch into the tree, or of the members into the body. Jesus is the Tree of Life, the true Vine, and we are the branches, just as the feet, tongue, arms, lungs and ears are the 'branches' of a human body.

Paul continues: 'God has arranged the parts in the body, every one of them, *just as He wanted them to be.*'[24] God is the sole Architect of the human body. It is He who decided on the number of our eyes, fingers, ribs, or arteries; and it is He who situated them in the body according to His supreme wisdom. So, likewise, *only God* knows how to build the body of Christ which is the church. It is He who designates our position *and our function* in His work. Happy is the man who allows the intelligence and will of God to decide what his function shall be in the body of Christ! What folly to try

(20) Eph. 1:21–23; Col. 1:18
(21) 1 Cor. 12:12
(22) 1 Cor. 12:27
(23) As in Jn. 15:5 and Rom. 11:16–24
(24) 1 Cor. 12:18

and force God to bestow on us a function or 'gift' that He doesn't intend for us!

The spiritual gifts

There are *three principal passages* in the New Testament concerning spiritual gifts: Romans 12:3–8; 1 Corinthians 12–14 (these three chapters are a single passage and must be studied together, as a whole); and, finally, Ephesians 4:1–16. To these may be added the brief passage in 1 Pet. 4:10–11. If you want to obtain a true and balanced understanding of the subject, you need to read all these passages right through, study all the material contained in them very carefully, and then compare them.

There are, in all, four 'lists' of spiritual gifts: Romans 12:6–8; 1 Corinthians 12:8–10 and 28; and Ephesians 4:11. These lists are all different, and there are unquestionably many other gifts which are not mentioned in them. Think, for example, of the spiritual gift of that believer who wrote the words of the hymn: 'Just as I am . . . I come', through which tens of thousands of souls have been saved. Yet there is no mention of such a gift in these four 'lists'. It is quite clear that they are not meant to be exhaustive, but rather representative.

As a matter of fact, God's thought as expressed by the Apostle Paul is very clear. In 1 Corinthians 12, basing his teaching on the analogy of the body and its members, he teaches the following truths:

'*There are varieties of gifts*, but the same Spirit.'[25] That is evident, for whoever saw a body composed of just one or two organs? As, for example, a mere tongue or one enormous ear! That would be monstrous. Thus, in the church, God wants a variety of gifts, and each one is necessary. They are complementary to one another.

'All the members do not have the same function.' We have 'gifts *that differ* according to the grace given us.'[26] What could be clearer than that?

'The Spirit apportions to each one individually *as He wills*' (or, 'just as He determines' NIV).[27] He is the sovereign; He

(25) 1 Cor. 12:4
(26) Rom. 12:4–6
(27) 1 Cor. 12:11

knows better than we do the needs of the church He is
building, and He knows how He can best use us to meet
those needs. It is not for us to dictate our wishes to Him in
this matter.

'To each is given the manifestation of the Spirit *for the
common good*.' [28] This shows us the true purpose of spiritual
gifts. The Spirit bestows a gift upon you in order that you
may be useful to other people, serve the church, win souls,
and make Christ known to the world. The gift is for the good
of everybody, not for your own personal satisfaction. The
finger, the eye, the foot do not exist for themselves, but for
the whole body. A finger, operating independently from the
rest of the body, is meaningless.

The members of Christ receive a variety of gifts in order
that the church may be edified, that is, built up. See also
Ephesians 4:12-16 where this truth is developed in depth. All
this means that, by the gift of His choice, the Spirit of God
qualifies you to serve God in the way He wishes, in the way He
can best use you to help your brothers and to bring lost souls
to Christ.

'The best gifts'

'*God has appointed* in the church *first* apostles, *second*
prophets, *third* teachers, *then* healers, etc.'[29] Not only is it
God who decides on our particular functions in the church,
but it is He also who decides their relative value. For the
Apostle Paul, the various gifts of the Spirit have varying
degrees of importance. There are some which he evidently
considers indispensable, and these he puts at the head of the
list, and it is these he tells us to seek after.

'His gifts were that some should be *apostles*, some *prophets*,
some *evangelists*, some *pastors* and *teachers* . . . for building
up the body of Christ.'[30] The church needs all kinds of gifts,
but no church can succeed, nor even exist for very long,
without these five particular gifts. Let us accept with gratitude
whatever additional gifts God is pleased to grant His people;
but we need to pray earnestly that He will provide us with an
abundance of these five essential functions.

(28) 1 Cor. 12:7
(29) 1 Cor. 12:28–30
(30) Eph. 4:11–12 (RSV)

The five indispensable gifts

1. *Apostle*, in Greek, means 'a man sent on a job' and corresponds to the Latin 'missionary'. The church has a terrible need of such pioneers to plant the good news of Christ where it is not known. The twelve Apostles are no longer on earth, nor can they be replaced by anyone else, for their essential function was to transmit faithfully all they had heard and seen of Jesus[31]; and this they have done in the writings of the New Testament. This cannot, of course, be repeated. But in the sense that Barnabas, Silas, and others are called apostles in the New Testament, that is, *missionaries* – men really sent by God – we do need apostles, thousands of them.

2. *Prophet*, in Greek, means 'mouthpiece' or 'spokesman'. The prophet of Israel spoke in the name of his God, and spent his life calling the people of God back to their Lord and to His Word[32]; he warned or encouraged them according to their attitude and condition[33]. The Christian prophet is likewise the man who is continually bringing us back to the Word of God. He is the moral or spiritual 'conscience' of the church. He is God's 'sentinel'[34]. He sees more clearly than other men because he knows the Scriptures and is intimate with God in prayer. He is gifted with spiritual intuition, but his message is based on the Word of God.

3. *Evangelist*, in Greek, means 'a man who brings good news', by whatever means. An evangelist is not necessarily gifted as a public speaker; he may have quite a different approach to souls. There are scores of ways of evangelising, though the Good News is ever the same. We are all called upon to evangelise, though we do not all have the *gift* of the evangelist; to him God has granted a special facility for the task, whereas we may have quite different abilities given us.

4. *Pastor*, in Greek, means 'shepherd'. The shepherd's job is to (a) *protect* the flock, taking special care of the weak and young; (b) *feed* the flock, ensuring they get good Bible

(31) Mk. 3:13–14; Acts 1:21–22
(32) 2 Chron. 36:15–16; Jer. 35:15
(33) 1 Cor. 14:3 (Greek: 'he speaks "edification", both warning and encouragement')
(34) Ezek. 33:7

teaching, even if he has to get someone else to provide it.[35]

5. *Teacher*. This is the man who not only acquires a deep and systematic knowledge of Bible truth, but has the gift of communicating it effectively to others. He lays the foundation for the church's life and action.[36]

What church can afford to do without these five surpassing gifts? They are 'top priority'. No gift can compare with these.

'*Earnestly desire the best gifts*.'[37] In this sentence, Paul sums up his whole attitude to spiritual gifts. He tells us to aim as high as possible. We must not judge our brothers with a gift other than our own; but it is up to each of us to ask God for the very best that He has for us individually – a gift that 'bears fruit', especially in souls saved.

Concerning these five gifts I have just mentioned, you sometimes hear people say that they, or some of them, are 'natural', as opposed to the 'spiritual' gifts. It is true that much preaching is tragically 'natural', the fruit of mere academic scholarship or of a psychological instinct. But the true teacher, pastor, prophet, or evangelist is deeply inspired by the Holy Spirit in his Ministry. Was Moses' gift merely 'natural' when he wrote Deuteronomy? Or that of the author of the Epistle to the Hebrews? Both these men were 'teachers'. Oh, may God send us men inspired of His Spirit for *all* His work! Why, the early Church insisted on having men filled with the Spirit *even to serve at the widows' tables*![38] We need to get back to this primitive concept of Christian service.

How do you discover your gift?

To begin with, try everything! Be ready to do anything at all for God; sweep out the preaching-hall, distribute gospels and tracts, do door-to-door work, join Bible study circles, visit the sick, help the poor and the aged, gain the children's interest, get hold of the young people. In short, give your unselfish help and do good wherever you can.

(35) Jn. 21:15–17; Acts 20:28–31; 1 Pet. 5:1–4
(36) Acts 20:26–27
(37) 1 Cor. 12:31
(38) Acts 6:1–3

Soon, in one way or another, the Spirit of God will begin to show you how He really wants to use you, in what way you can be most useful to Him. He will certainly use your natural capacities. Are you a poet? A guitarist? A bricklayer? Do you know how to gain the confidence of teenagers? Are you gifted with children? Your Creator knew all this about you even before the world existed; it is not for nothing that He has made you as you are. Only, do not make the mistake of confusing 'natural capacity' with 'spiritual gift'. There very frequently is a *relationship* between the two, for God uses our whole being. There is also, however, a real *difference*.

Paul, for example, before his conversion, had a magnificent brain and he knew the Old Testament Scriptures very well; nevertheless he demolished the church of God. But when he met with the living Christ on the Damascus road, he broke with sin, with his past, and with the world – even with the religious world. Not only was he baptised physically, but God also 'baptised' his personality *with its natural capacities*. He died with Christ in that spiritual baptism. God then rebuilt his mind, his intuition, his very personality. I believe that the methodical reasoning of the Epistle to the Romans is unequalled in the literature of the world; but it is reasoning utterly inspired by the Holy Spirit. Paul's brain, purified by God, became the instrument of the wisdom of God. Yet it was still Paul's brain! The 'natural' was absorbed into the 'spiritual' and transformed in the process.

You are a unique being whom God is integrating into the body of Christ according to His unfathomable wisdom. He is designing a job for you, a function that will enable you to serve and glorify Him in the most effective way possible. So why not enter into a positive agreement with Him about your future? He will not disappoint you. He will astonish you. But you must be ready for a tough apprenticeship!

Must we accept the tragic facts?

In these pages I have sought to show what the church really is, the true church as Jesus designed it, and as the Apostles brought it into being. It is a miracle of the Holy Spirit. You need to keep this vision always before your eyes and ask God to bring it to pass in so far as you are concerned.

But alas, we don't have to look very far before discovering that there are many churches and groups, even calling themselves biblical, which are far from this apostolic ideal. Our hearts are smitten with grief as we come up against sacrosanct structures that kill the joyous spontaneity of the Spirit, forms of prayer and worship that freeze our faith, and rigid doctrinal concepts that rule out all possibility of spiritual progress. Or else, a sort of spiritual 'free for all', where people do and say all sorts of things that simply cannot be justified from Scripture. What attitude should we adopt in such cases?

First of all, and above all, we must love. If the people concerned are true children of God who love the Lord Jesus and recognise the inspiration and divine authority of the Scriptures, we should look upon them as being precious to God's heart, and so precious to ours also. It may even be that God considers them to be of more spiritual value than we are. So long as God wants you to stay in such an environment, do so in the same spirit and with the same love as Jesus would show. 'Christ loved the Church and gave Himself for her' – in spite of her imperfections. [39] Do all you can to bring help and blessing where God puts you.

It is even, at times, a useful discipline to have to put up with a difficult and unreasonable yoke. God can use it to teach you patience, compassion, and humility. Who knows? God may perhaps use you in such a situation to bring about true spiritual revival.

God, however, does not want you to waste all your life in an unprofitable situation. In the end you must, like the Apostles, obey God rather than men.[40] Sooner or later, and preferably sooner, God will surely open up a road that leads you to something worthwhile. Ask Him unceasingly to show you His will. You can't hope to make spiritual progress simply by avoiding difficulties; you must confront them courageously and honestly. Yet God wants at all costs to use you; and if He cannot do it where you are, then He assuredly has something else for you. It is better to start distributing literature all on your own, to reach those who know nothing of Christ, than to squander your life in church activities that lead

(39) Eph. 5:25
(40) Acts 5:29

nowhere. God hasn't called you to live in a spiritual cemetery. You need to think also of the souls that God, I hope, will save through your witness. No one would surely dream of putting his baby in a refrigerator, and certainly not in a coffin! Neither do you want to dump your spiritual 'baby' in a church like that. It is true, we all have to serve an apprentice-ship, and that is never easy; but nobody is expected to stay an apprentice all his life. You must go on to become a fully-qualified workman. God is in desperate need of such men and women, and He doesn't believe in wasting them. Ask God to find you a real spiritual job where you can serve Him effectively and bear fruit that lasts.

Supposing you find yourself in a good church

It may be that you have the immense privilege of being in a truly spiritual church, where the Christians love each other and evangelise, and where the Bible is faithfully studied. That is really marvellous! It is a precious favour from God. But remember two things:

Jesus said that it is more blessed to give than to receive.[41] There are two kinds of 'Christians', the givers and the grabbers! The joyous and the grumblers! The church can do without spiritual parasites or the spiritually unemployed. It already has enough to do with its babies that can still only suck and cry. The church desperately needs members who bring a blessing to everyone else. If you are full of the Holy Spirit, you will bring the presence of God into the church with you. You will give generously of your friendship, your faith, your money and your time. If, on the contary, you go there only for what you can get, only to grasp, then you will finally be disappointed.

Secondly, the perfect church does not exist on earth. According to our attitude we are ourselves blessed or disappointed. Keep yourself day and night from every inclination to accuse and to criticise. Jesus utterly forbids us to speak evil of one another, most of all behind the other's back.[42] No, on the contrary, pray day and night for your church and its leaders.

(41) Acts 20:35
(42) On this subject you should read Matt. 7:1–5; 18:15; Rom. 14:1–15:7; 1 Cor. 13

If it is possible for you to choose your church, do so very carefully and with much prayer. Do not commit yourself lightly; but when you do commit yourself, do so with your whole heart. Choose a church which is faithful to the Scriptures and also full of the Holy Spirit; that is to say, a group where Jesus is really present. It doesn't matter if it is small or poor. If Christ is there, you are richer than all the banks in the world combined. Besides, in a small church you will find a purpose in being alive; you will be a valuable and important member of the family; you will have a real contribution to make. If, on the other hand, you are in a very large church you will probably be submerged in an anonymous mass – which is very bad for your spiritual health. You become lazy and useless, or just frustrated.

What if the church is unfaithful?

If the church does not recognise the deity of Christ, nor the absolute authority of the Word of God, nor the new birth by faith, I don't see what you are doing there. I don't think your place is in that church. What have you in common with God's enemies? The fact of sporting the label 'Christian' or 'church' does not cancel out the enormity of their sin of rejecting all that is most precious to the heart of God.

But perhaps you will answer me that you want to stay there as a witness. A witness? Yes, of course, we are all called to be witnesses everywhere. But as a member? That is a totally different matter. Read 2 Corinthians 6:14-18. 'What has a believer in common with an unbeliever? . . . What is there in common between light and darkness?' You just do not belong there. However, when you leave them, do even that with love.

What if you are all alone?

Not everyone has the privilege of sharing Christ with other believers. There are some of His disciples who are painfully isolated by circumstances: I am thinking of those who are quite alone in a whole region hostile to Christ; or of the young man, in so many countries, doing his military service; or the girl who is the only Christian in her boarding-school. Perhaps you are the only believer in your village or town. Think, too, of our brothers in those countries which are spiritually starved, and especially those believers who are in prison for their faith. And what a lot of them there are! We need to pray for them day and night. Yet we do not need to cross seas or frontiers to discover children of God who are terribly isolated. What are we doing to encourage and help them?

It may be you yourself are one of these solitary Christians. In that case, you have my deep sympathy. You can be sure, however, that God will never forsake you; He will give you *special* grace in these special circumstances. Apply yourself all the more to prayer and the Word of God. Actually, you are not alone. If God is with you, you possess greater resources than the whole world itself. If God is for you, who can be against you?[43]

But for those who are in fact able to join with others of God's children, His commandment is positive: 'We are not to forsake the assembling of ourselves together.'[44] We owe it to our brothers and sisters, and at the same time we ourselves have need of them. In reality, we are all intimately linked up through Christ in heaven.

You are not alone!

(43) Rom. 8:31–39
(44) Heb. 10:25

11

YOU CANNOT KEEP GOD JUST FOR YOURSELF

*The fourth principle:
Witness, or the outreach of faith*

So far we have examined the different ways of receiving and maintaining a life of fullness. But this life is not an end in itself. Rather, it is a means of taking us further still!

The electric cable only exists in order to transmit the current. The river does not keep the living waters it receives; it has to give them all away. Thus the whole of the life of fullness issues in sacrifice, in the giving of yourself; or rather, in communicating to others the Spirit of Christ entrusted to you. *If we do not pass on our spiritual life, it will evaporate or stagnate.* Like the manna, which perished when the Israelites tried to keep it. Like the Dead Sea. The outreach, or out-working, of your faith means giving out to a lost world what you receive from God. Life, essentially, is *giving*. That is the culmination of faith. Without it, faith is sterile.

We believe in Christ because we have come face to face with His sacrifice. It is the *grace* of God that has convinced us. The word *grace* means, in the Greek original, *generosity*. We have been won by the indescribable generosity of God in Christ. The Love with which God has flooded our heart becomes the motive force of our entire life; and it is this same love which the people around us need to experience through us. Nothing else will convince the world of the authenticity of our message, for this divine love is *the only thing that the devil cannot counterfeit*. The love of God is revealed in the gift of Himself; and He can only reveal Himself through us as we also give ourselves.

There are, in fact, *three ways by which we can give ourselves*, or rather, give Christ to men.

First, we give by our witness

Jesus said: 'Everyone who acknowledges me before men,
I also will acknowledge him before my Father who is in
heaven; but whoever denies me before men, I also will deny
him before my Father.'[1]

And again: 'The Spirit of truth will bear witness of Me,
and you also will bear witness.'[2]

The whole of the New Testament insists that we must
witness to men concerning Christ. We cannot be disciples of
Christ, in the world that crucified Him, without identifying
ourselves with Him openly and taking a stand for Him. We
are saved when we first identify ourselves with Jesus before
God, and when God Himself in reply identifies us with Him.
But this identification cannot remain secret. If our faith is
really the work of His Spirit, it cannot be dumb. We are the
witnesses of Christ before a world that does not know Him
and cannot know Him except through our witness.

A witness can only say what he actually knows, what he has
in fact seen and heard. All that we can say to the world about
Jesus is what we actually know of Him in our experience. A
'secondhand' witness convinces no one; it simply does not
have the ring of truth. We don't have to work up or 'manu-
facture' our witness; God expects us to witness courageously
to the *truth*, however simple, however limited may be our
experience of Christ. When we do, He guarantees us the
support of His Spirit of *truth* to back up our feeble witness.[3]
If I cease to be known as a disciple of Christ, the witness of the
Spirit is quenched; I lose His fullness until I put this matter
right.

The Lord calls us 'the light of the world' and 'the salt of the
earth'.[4] A few grains of salt transform the flavour of the
cooking! Even a little candle can be seen from a long way off.
Jesus did not say: 'You ought to be the light of the world',
but: 'You *are* the light of the world'. Believe that. Count on
it. *Rely therefore on His Spirit to witness convincingly through
you to men.*

(1) Mt. 10:32–33
(2) Jn. 15:26–27
(3) Jn. 15:26–27
(4) Mt. 5:13–14

Not a paper cross

Obviously, it is hard to take a stand for Jesus Christ in this world; sooner or later it will bring persecution. Jesus never hid this truth from us. He said emphatically that we cannot be His disciples if we refuse to follow Him to the point of carrying the cross too – which means, going to our own execution! But what is infinitely harder than even that is the grief and frustration which comes as the result of our failure to witness. When we take a stand for Christ in this world, the Spirit of God fills us. At that point it is He who witnesses and loves through us, who crowns our suffering with His heavenly joy, His peace, His satisfaction. A Christian *cannot be happy* if he hides his faith.

Are you afraid to suffer?

The true Christian is like a plant created to live on the mountain summits, or in the fiercest desert, a flower that thrives marvellously in suffering and adversity. Those unspeakably beautiful gentians of such unearthly blue, that grow on the high Alps, are not found down on the plains. You can't produce that effect in your kitchen garden. To have those colours they must brave the appalling winter storms, the intense ice and snow, the knife-like winds, and, above all, the altitude. They need an air that is rare and pure, that civilisation cannot pollute. The Christian is made for a life of utter purity, close to God's blue heaven, in the dazzle of God's sheer light. This is how God develops the character of Christ in us.

The Christian who has not suffered tends to be hard on others whose sufferings he cannot understand. Under his brash exterior he is often quite feeble in spirit himself, even superficial, lacking the tough resistance and also the humility of the martyr. If there is one thing of which we may be proud in eternity, in the kingdom of God, it will surely be the scars of the sufferings we have endured for love of Christ.

Secondly, we give by our good works

Paul said that 'we were created in Christ Jesus *to do good works*';[5] that is, good deeds. In other words, God has saved us for the very purpose of doing all the good we possibly can.

(5) Eph. 2:10

Again Paul said: 'Brothers, *do not get tired of doing good*.'[6]; He said that the spiritual Christian is *'ready for all good deeds'*;[7] he urges those who have believed in God to be 'careful *to maintain good deeds*', [8] that is, to keep doing good; to express the love of God to their fellow-men.

Peter summed up the life of the Lord Jesus Christ in these words: 'He went about *doing good*'.[9] If our Master spent His life in doing good, then we, His disciples, should do the same. Besides, it is by doing good that we at last convince the world of the authenticity of our witness. There are a thousand ways of doing good. We don't need to waste our powers, our money or our time on a merely political or exclusively social cause. But every Christian should radiate goodness around him; every church, each of Christ's teams, should do good by every means possible. Yet all our good works should be done in the name of the Lord Jesus and thus associated with our witness. They are then a good advertisement for the gospel; otherwise they are simply a drain on our resources and lead to no positive end. Of course, such good works really cost us something, but that is what finally convinces people of our sincerity. The Lord's brother James said: 'As the body without the spirit is dead, so also faith without works [that is, deeds] is dead'.[10]

We need, however, to distinguish what God calls 'good works' from what He means by 'dead works'. 'Good works' are the mature and spontaneous flowering of the life of the Spirit within us, the expression of our new-found love for God; whereas 'dead works' are the repugnant attempts of our old nature to 'buy off' God or impress men with the assumption that we are really worth something. They are the bitter fruit of our ego's effort to appear something other than we are. They stem from pride and self-interest, not from sacrificial love.

Thirdly, we give by our work for God

In this world, the man who doesn't work ends up losing

(6) 2 Thess. 3:13
(7) 2 Tim. 2:21
(8) Tit. 3:8
(9) Acts 10:38
(10) Jas. 2:26

all purpose in life; he degenerates. To remain spiritually 'unemployed' is just as dangerous or more so. You need a positive spiritual occupation, a definite job of work. If you haven't got one, go and ask God to take you on!

There are innumerable ways of serving God, but all work for Him must have as its real goal the evangelisation of the world. If you are aiming at any other purpose than that, you are throwing most of your time and strength into a bottomless pit. A living church has all kinds of activities, but they should all have as their real objective the evangelisation of the nations, *and especially of those that do not as yet possess the New Testament.* No other work can even compare with this in importance. If the church loses this vision, it is on a slippery downward track. Christ died for all men and He insists that we inform every single one. It is the least we can do for mankind. Happy is the believer who realises this and the church that puts it into practice!

As I have said, we do not all have the 'gift of an evangelist', but we are all called to evangelise! Knowing how hard it is for us to do this on our own, God intended that we should do it if possible together with our fellow-believers, on a 'team' basis. Jesus, when He ascended to heaven, leaving those eleven young men, His Apostles, on the Mount of Olives, committed to them the imperative, huge responsibility of evangelising the whole world. I sometimes call these eleven 'Christ's football team'! Every church should have, or be, such a team. Paul and the other Apostles fully grasped the supreme value of the Christ-made team; for it was by this means that they filled their world with new churches!

In a football team, not everybody is a striker! But, if each man plays his specific part, the team as a whole can score the goals that win the match. So, in the church, we do not all have the special ability of the evangelist; we have, as Paul says, many different gifts and functions. But each of us has something positive to contribute, and, by the concerted action of all, the world can and will be evangelised. The goalkeeper is just as necessary as the striker, even though he never scores a goal. If God gives you what seems to be an undistinguished job, you can be sure that it is an invaluable contribution to Christ's final victory. It is a necessary part of the whole scope of God's action. What a reward there will be – and you can be sure that it will be shared out among the whole team!

Jesus says that there is 'more joy in heaven over one sinner who repents' than . . . over ninety-nine Christians who are merely 'good', but who are not winning souls![11] Whatever work God gives you, do not miss the absolutely heavenly joy of leading sinners to Christ, and of putting the New Testament into the hands of some of the two thousand million human beings, or more, who are still without it. May God *multiply* your life!

(11) Lk. 15:3–7; Mt. 18:12–14

Part IV

THIS LIFE
ISN'T EVERYTHING

12

CERTAINTY OF CERTAINTIES: JESUS IS COMING BACK!

You were made to live in God's open spaces

This world will disappear. The universe will cease to be. 'But he who does the will of God remains forever.'[1] The Christian life is marvellous: it is a foretaste of heaven. Nevertheless it is spent in suffering. Peter goes so far as to say that it is to this that we have been called.[2] The word 'witness' in Greek is *martyros*, which means 'martyr' for us. Jesus never concealed this truth.

Faith is forged in suffering. Far from destroying it, suffering stimulates it. Through our pain, God is forming the elements of His new creation, the new scheme of things which will replace the tragic wreck of this world. He is preparing something of hitherto unimaginable beauty, which, tomorrow, will make us forever forget all our tears.[3]

We who belong to Christ are already a part of that new creation;[4] we no longer belong to this old world which is doomed to vanish away. Our new life is eternal, rooted in God Himself. As the gardener, at the coming of spring, transplants into the open air the shrubs and flowers he has so patiently cared for under glass all through the winter, so God, at the return of Christ, will transplant us into the kingdom of His Son. You will always be yourself; but instead of being cultivated under the cramped conditions of your present existence, you will be translated into that atmosphere, that element, for which you have been conceived. You will ever live in the immediate presence of God. And that presence is heaven.

(1) 1 Jn. 2:17
(2) 1 Pet. 2:21
(3) Rom. 8:18
(4) 2 Cor. 5:17

Another word that has lost its meaning!

'Heaven' ... marvellous, pitiful word, distorted by centuries of ignorance! The Middle Ages (and perhaps even our religious education) seem to have left us with the idea of a disembodied soul sitting on a cloud somewhere in outer space, endlessly strumming on a spiritual guitar!

As we get to know the Bible these absurdities fade out, and their place is taken by a dazzlingly beautiful symbolism through which our conscience comes to grips with reality.

Eternal life is essentially spiritual, otherwise it would be impossible for us to see God; but it is not necessarily divorced from the material universe. The Lord Jesus went away into the glory with the risen human body which the disciples had recognised as His own, and which bore the very scars of His crucifixion. Hebrews chapter 2 reminds us that He is still human even now, otherwise He would not be able to represent our human race before His Father's face as our High Priest. And the Bible insists that He is the same today and for ever.[5]

Heaven is not all that far from the earth!

Moreover, He is going to return to earth again. We read that His feet will again stand upon the Mount of Olives, from which He left earth at His ascension. We are going to meet Him, *but not as disembodied spirits*. We shall rise from the dead. In this connection, I recommend the reading of the fantastic fifteenth chapter of 1 Corinthians – a masterpiece of divine inspiration concerning the resurrection. As I conclude this book I can only allude to these things briefly. We should need several weeks together to study this subject in depth.

It is enough here to say that heaven, for us, is the presence of Jesus. Since He is God, Jesus is omnipresent in space and beyond the universe; yet all the prophets affirm that He will return to this very same earth where He was crucified.[6] Since we shall be with Him, it goes without saying that we shall be closely concerned with the earth during His reign, which is described in Revelation chapter 20 and in very many passages in the Old Testament prophecies. Jesus is going to reign over

(5) Heb. 13:8
(6) Zech. 14:3–4; Acts 1:11

the nations[7] and we shall of necessity be associated with Him in His reign, even though we may not all be called actually to rule.[8] Jesus gives very full teaching on this phase of our experience, and He, like His servant Paul, insists on the fact that our way of living now will determine the position which we shall occupy then.[9]

We are living for tomorrow

Our present life is only an anticipation. It is our 'school', where we are preparing for our 'university entrance' examination! I think of Christ's reign over the nations as our 'university course', when we shall certainly have the possibility, not only of further spiritual study, but also of putting into practice the results of our present experience.

Revelation chapter 20 speaks of a reign of Christ of a thousand years on this earth. A thousand years of divine university! Just imagine! And perhaps with enormous responsibilities, as Christ involves you in the fulfilling of His strategic purposes. At the end of this period you should be ready to take your 'degree' or even a 'doctorate' which will qualify you for some absolutely incredible job in the new creation! Do you realise? The more you know God, the more beauty you can create.

For God whispers in our ear the divine Word that the cosmos itself, including the earth, will be completely renewed. We do not know how; God keeps His secret; but that is the ultimate objective to which we are called. That is where we belong. And it is in that framework that we shall be able to develop to the uttermost the thought-process that God has implanted in us. Christ will then appear to us more radiant than ever in the midst of His new creation, as the work of His hands takes shape.

Think hard!

But if I waste my time now, if I squander the resources that God offers me today in Christ, if I neglect my present

(7) Pss. 47, 72, 96, 97, 98; Mic. 4:4; Zech. 14:16, 19, and countless other passages.
(8) 2 Tim. 2:11–13
(9) Lk. 19:11–27; 1 Cor. 3:11–15

responsibilities, how do you expect God to entrust me with the responsibilities of His kingdom? If, said Jesus, we are not faithful in the small things, who will entrust us with the things of eternal value?[10] At present the Lord is studying us searchingly; He is looking for the men to whom He can confide 'key posts' in His kingdom. The world as yet is governed by the devil and his angels; but at the return of Christ all that satanic hierarchy will be swept away, and there will remain a spiritual void behind the nations. God intends to fill it with those of His children who are faithful and competent in His service *now*. He has His eye on *you*.

The Lord Jesus, in the parable of the pounds, teaches that some believers will have a reward, that is, responsibilities in His kingdom; while others will lose theirs.[11] Paul teaches exactly the same thing.[12] We are *saved* by faith alone, but we shall be *judged* – by the Son of God – according to the use we have made of the faith which He gave us.[13]

And when Christ appears

'We shall *all* be changed, in a moment, in the twinkling of an eye'[14] and 'we shall be caught up together . . . in the clouds to meet the Lord'.[15] At that moment we shall see Him face to face,[16] and 'we shall be like Him'.[17] We shall be in eternity itself, facing the full reality of His presence. But we shall be there in our resurrection body, 'fully clothed' with true Christ-like humanity. And, in that eternal instant, at least two things will happen:

The Judgement-Seat of Christ.[18] In that flash of truth, when the incredible beauty and righteousness of Christ explode all fallacies, each of us will find his true spiritual level, and his real position, his function in the plan of Christ corresponding to that level. There will be no possibility then of making

(10) Lk. 16:10–12
(11) Lk. 19:11–27, esp. vv. 15–25
(12) 1 Cor. 3:11–15
(13) 2 Cor. 5:10; Rev. 2:23; 22:12
(14) 1 Cor. 15:52
(15) 1 Thes. 4:17
(16) 1 Cor. 13:12
(17) 1 Jn. 3:2
(18) Rom. 14:10

up for lost time; we shall be in time no longer. Our Judge will, thank God, be the One who poured out His blood for us on Calvary; nevertheless the Scriptures portray this experience as solemn in the highest degree. John says some of us may 'shrink from Him in shame at His coming'.[19] Will He say to you then: 'Enter into the joy of your Lord'?

It is supremely important that we should judge ourselves now, in advance, by the light of His Word, in anticipation of that day; for, as Paul says, 'if we judged ourselves truly, we should not be judged.'[20]

The Marriage of the Lamb[21] will follow the Judgement of the believer. God will openly recognise the union of Christ with His bride before the whole universe. We are that bride. As Boaz purchased the poor stranger, Ruth, to be his wife,[22] so Christ has bought us with His blood. What a moment, marvellous beyond words or imagination! Nothing will ever again come between Him and us. Are you ready?

(19) 1 Jn. 2:28
(20) 1 Cor. 11:31
(21) Rev. 19:6–9
(22) Ruth 4:9–10

THE END